naked PASTOR 101

cartoons by david hayward

nakedpastor101

Copyright © 2010 by David Hayward.
ISBN: 978-1453898413

All rights reserved. No part of this book may be used or reproduced in any manner whatsoever without written permission, except in the case of brief quotations embodied in critical articles or reviews.

Published 2010
Design by Tash McGill, Sola Fida Ltd.
www.solafida.co.nz

dedication

To Lisa, Joshua, Jesse and Casile. Fellow pilgrims.
I love you.

acknowledgements

I want to thank my **family** who has put up with me for so long talking about doing this but never getting around to it. But their voice, along with the following voices, became my cloud of witnesses pushing me onward.

I want to thank all the **fans** of nakedpastor. It is for you that this book has finally come to life. It is a pleasure to serve you.

I want to thank the **church**, especially Rothesay Vineyard. It was in your midst where I learned how to be.

Thanks to my friend **Jon Hallewell** who succeeded me as pastor of my last church. He helped me to conceive the idea for this book and get it out of my mind and onto paper.

Finally, I want to thank **Tash McGill** who designed this book. We met in Haiti, where I became acquainted with her designing skills. I'm thankful that because of technology we could work together even though she's on the other side of the world. Thanks Tash! You're amazing.

nakedpastor101

about the author

David Hayward graduated from Central Bible College in Springfield, MO., with his B.A. in Bible and Theology. He then graduated with his Masters of Theological Studies from Gordon-Conwell Theological Seminary in Boston.

He completed another Masters, this time of Ministry and Religion at Presbyterian College, McGill University, Montreal, Canada. He was ordained into the ministry of the Presbyterian Church in Canada in 1988. He has been the pastor of several churches, including the Vineyard, for over 25 years.

David met Lisa, the love of his life, in college. They married in 1980 and have three children, Joshua, Jesse and Casile. They live near Saint John, New Brunswick, Canada.

He is an artist working mainly with watercolor and ink on paper. He also works with woodcuts, stone sculpture and other media. His gallery can be found here: *www.haywardart.etsy.com*

You can purchase prints of his cartoons in his online cartoon gallery: *www.nakedpastor.etsy.com.*

Many of the original cartoons within this book are also available for purchase. Please contact David if you are interested: *haywardart@gmail.com*

Check out the blog that started all this: *nakedpastor.com.* From there you can connect with him through other social networking media.

All the images in this book are copyright: dhayward, 2010, aka "nakedpastor".

nakedpastor101

introduction

I started blogging in 2005. I began with "churchpundit". I liked the name, but it didn't convey what I wanted my blog to be about. I eventually came up with "nakedpastor". After some auctioning, I aquired the domain name. It hasn't been an easy name to bear. I often have to explain what it means. It's just about a pastor baring his soul. Nothing else.

Because of the name, many people can't access the site where they would like. It is filtered out of work places, schools, colleges, public libraries, and other such venues. It is also blocked by most personal accountability software at home. I've almost changed the name to circumvent this traffic problem, but nakedpastor has grown into its own brand.
So I've decided to stick with it. Besides… I like it!

Early in the life of nakedpastor I tried cartooning. I am an artist, but I mainly do landscapes in watercolor. I eventually came upon a style that was uniquely mine. The humor cuts across many lines and boundaries, pleasing some and offending others. But by the way my cartoons circulate around the web, I concluded that they are striking a chord with enough people that it warrants a collection.

These are what I consider my 101 best black and white cartoons. If you follow nakedpastor you will recognize 91 of them. There are 10 exclusive to this book that won't be seen on the blog. I have a collection of my best color cartoons coming out shortly.

Some fans will notice that certain themes have been omitted from this collection, such as my rants against church vision and mission statements, cartoons addressing the gay issue, as well as most of my cartoons dealing with money, the holidays, and my R-rated ones. They'll be coming along soon.

So, open the pages and enjoy. I hope they speak to you in meaningful ways. I have kept my commentary to a minimum, trusting that the cartoons will speak for themselves, as they should.

David Hayward, August 2010.

nakedpastor101

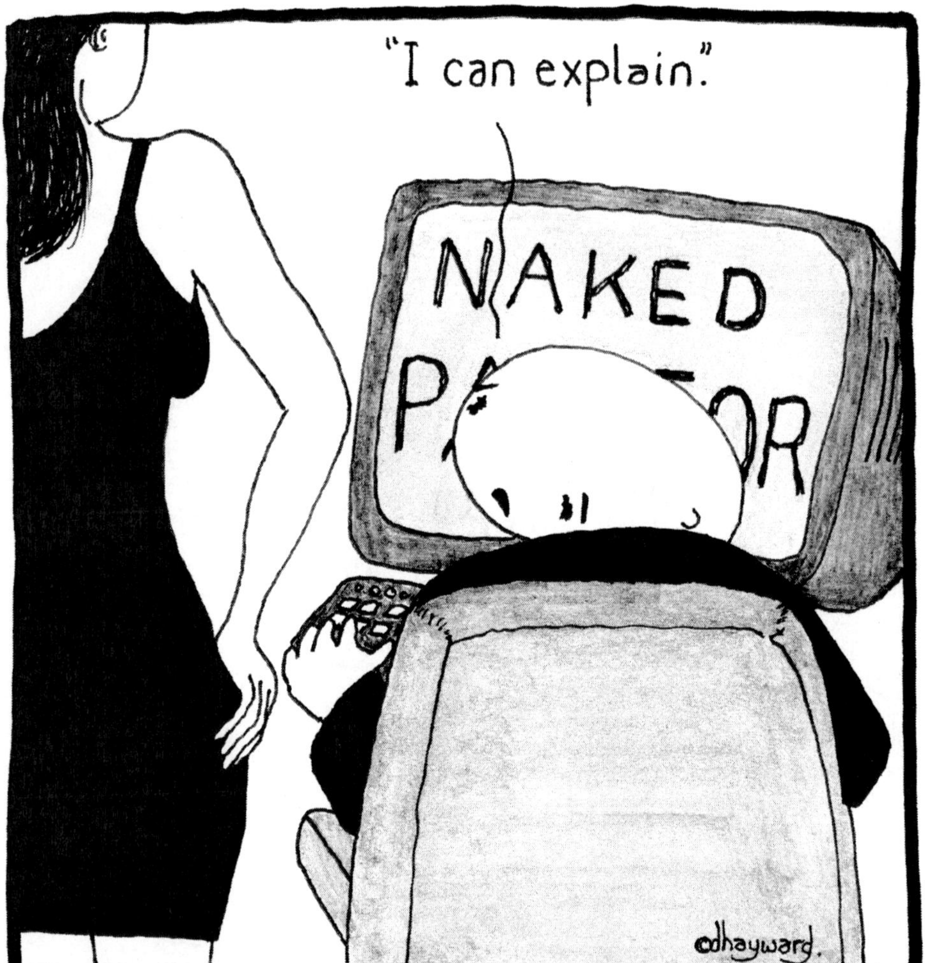
"I can explain."
NAKED
P OR
©dhayward.

I've received many emails from people "caught" reading the nakedpastor blog and having to explain that it wasn't porn.

nakedpastor101 002

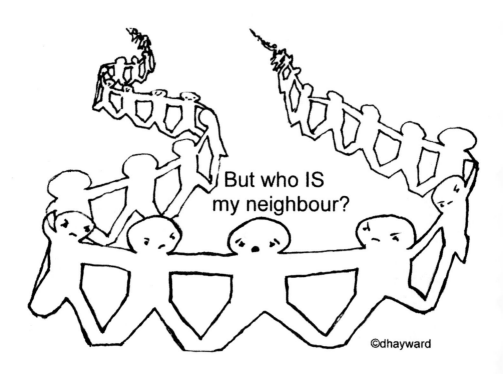

Some people just don't get the connections.

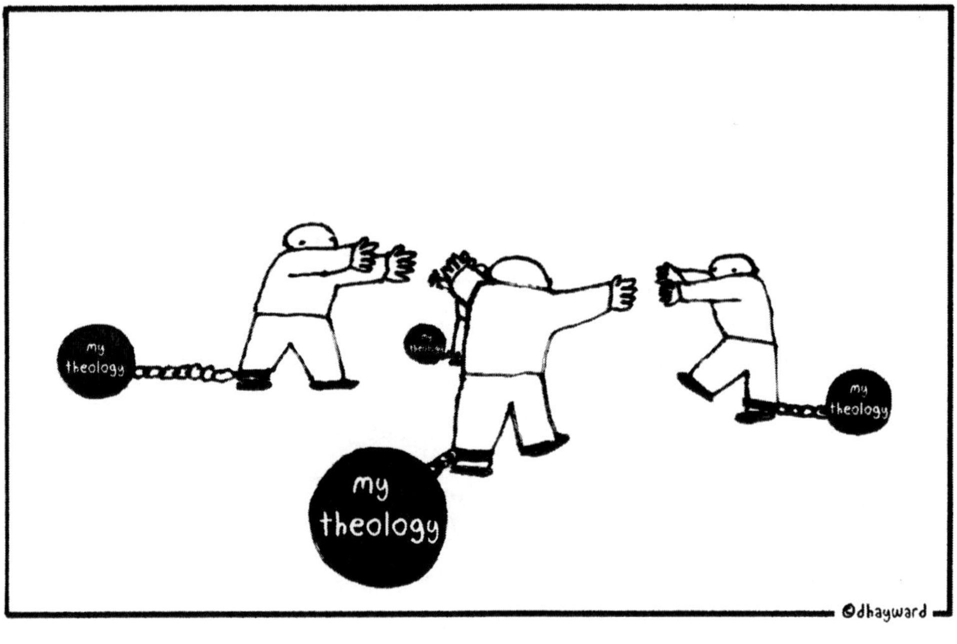
my theology
my theology
my theology
my theology
©dhayward

004

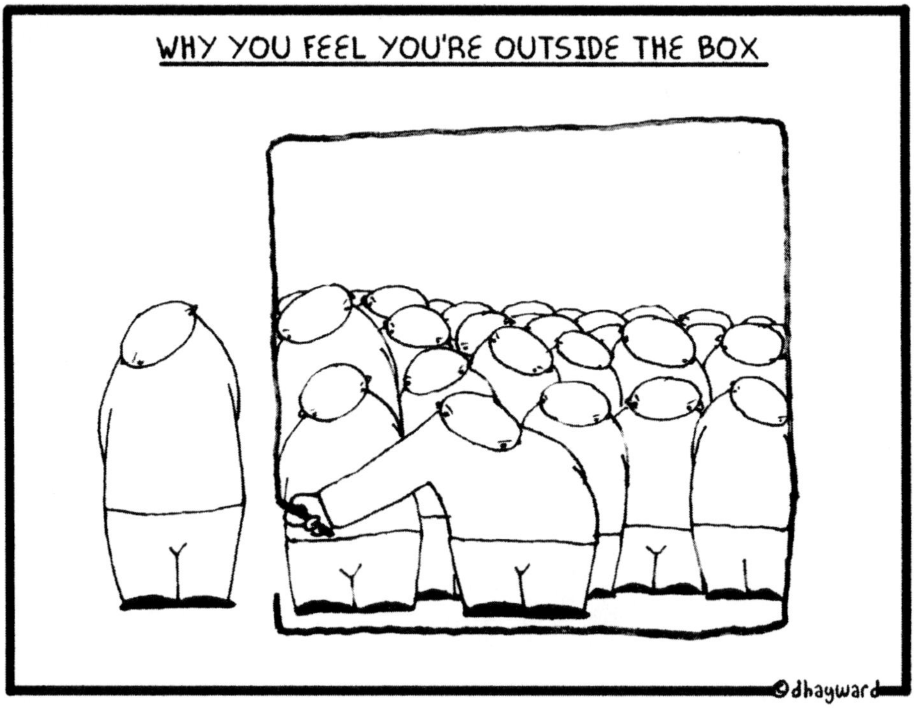
WHY YOU FEEL YOU'RE OUTSIDE THE BOX
©dhayward

I know a lot of people who've experienced this. A line is drawn and they find themselves on the other side.

TOO MANY FIRST STONES

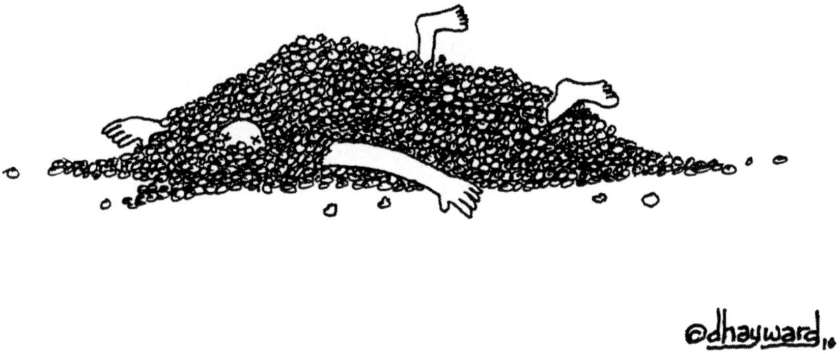
©dhayward16

René Girard, in his important book I See Satan Fall Like Lightning, writes, "the first stone is decisive because it is the most difficult to throw. Why is it the most difficult to throw? Because it is the only one without a model." Someone here decided to throw the first stone. Once it was thrown, the rest followed.

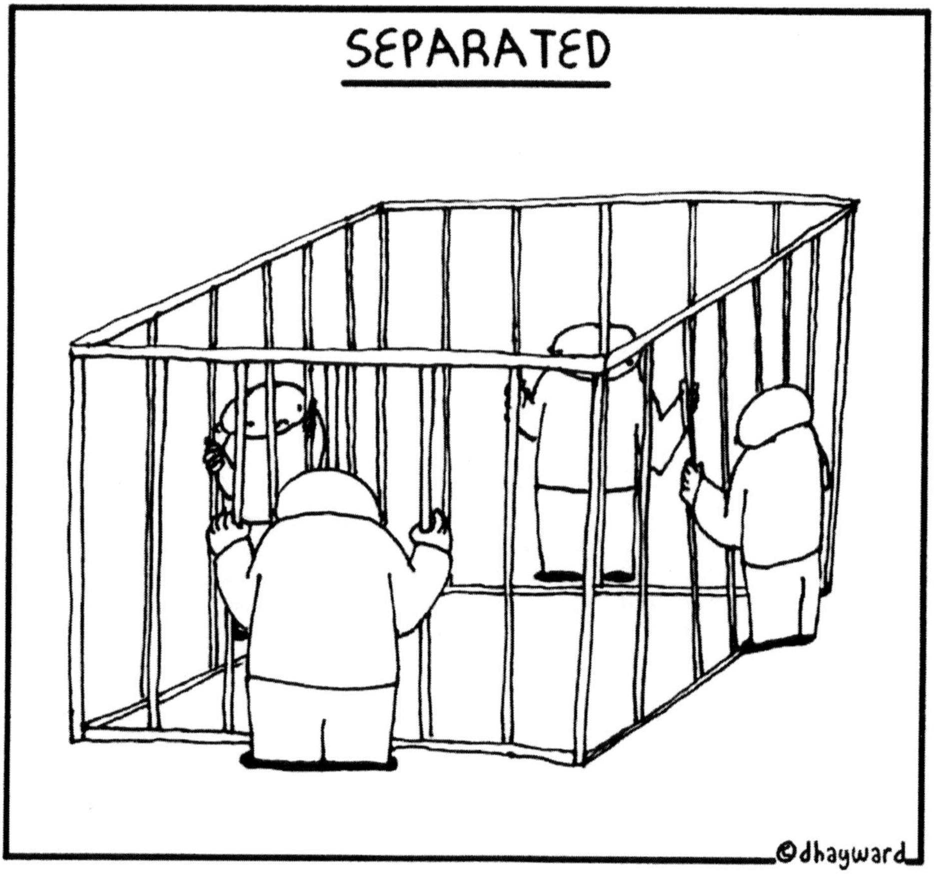
SEPARATED
©dhayward

Sometimes reconciliation and unity is just a walk around the corner. Those things which separate us are illusions. They feel and look and behave real, but they can all be circumvented.

007

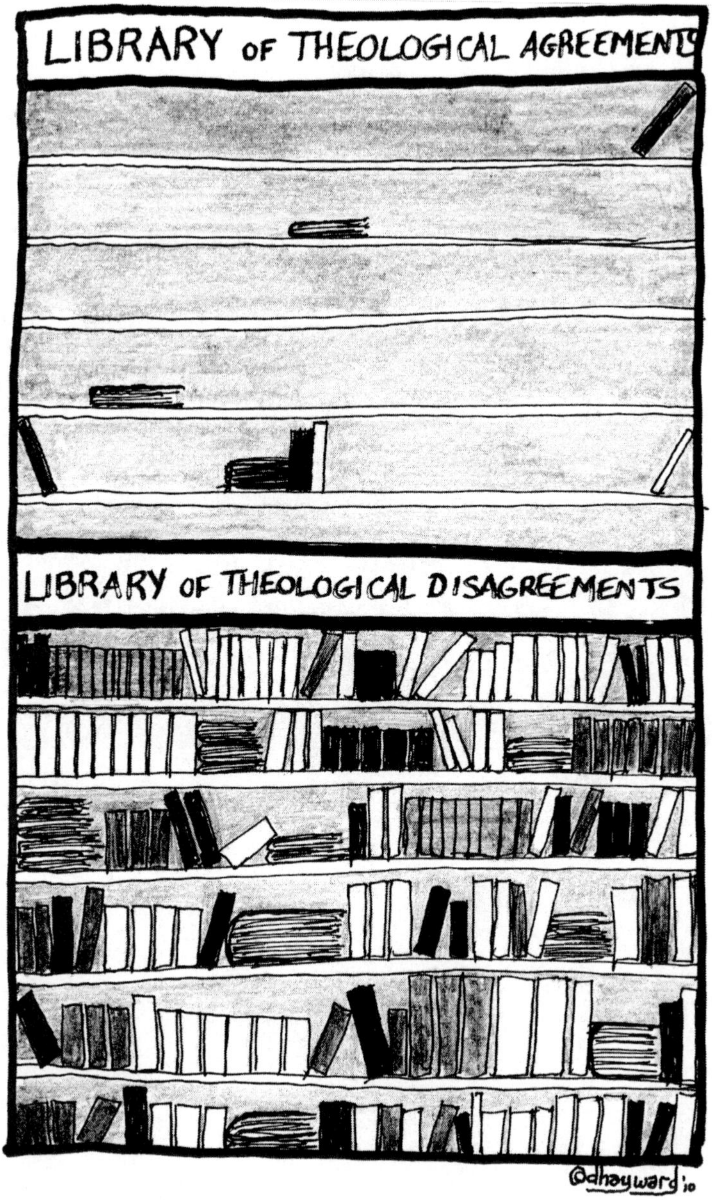
LIBRARY OF THEOLOGICAL AGREEMENTS
LIBRARY OF THEOLOGICAL DISAGREEMENTS
@dhayward '10

I had to put at least some books on the shelves for the library of theological agreements. But I might've been generous.

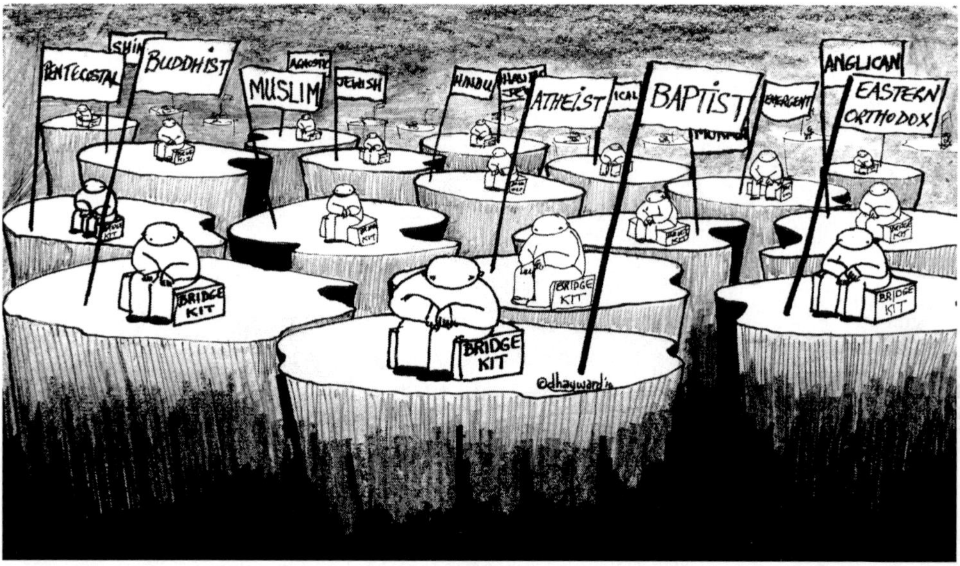
PENTECOSTAL
BUDDHIST
AGNOSTIC
MUSLIM
JEWISH
HINDU
ATHEIST
BAPTIST
EMERGENT
ANGLICAN
EASTERN ORTHODOX
BRIDGE KIT
BRIDGE KIT
BRIDGE KIT
BRIDGE KIT
©dhayward'10

We are all sitting on the means to repair relationships. We all have the means for reconciliation. Unity is a reality that can be made manifest.

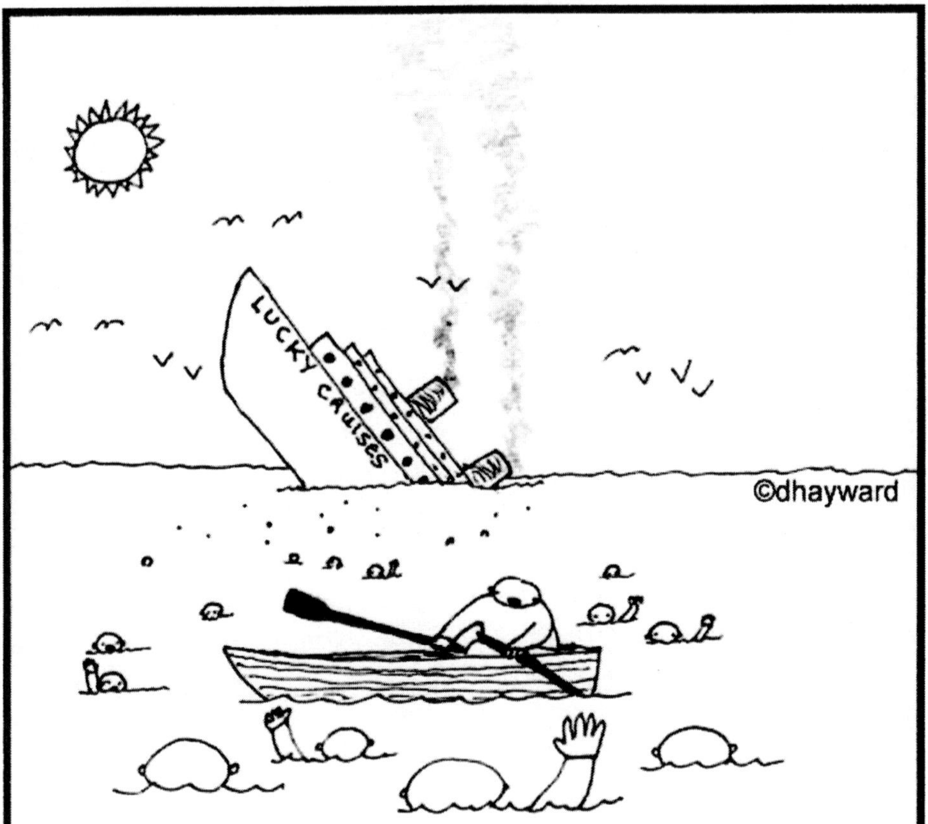
LUCKY CRUISES
©dhayward

I'm really sorry everyone, but I only fellowship with people of like faith.

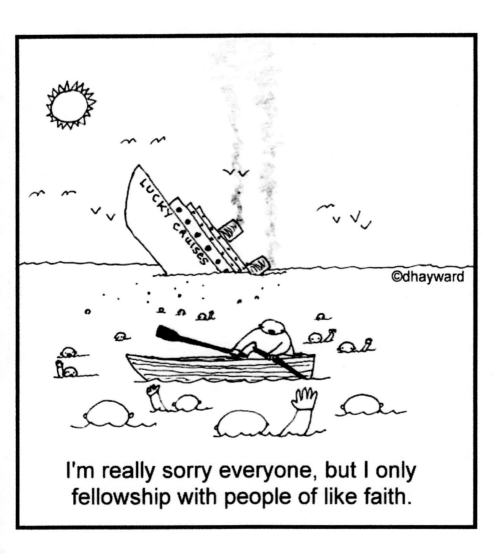

I've been a part of fellowships that required we only fellowship with people of like faith so that we wouldn't be contaminated with heresy or sin. I wonder how far we'd be willing to carry that.

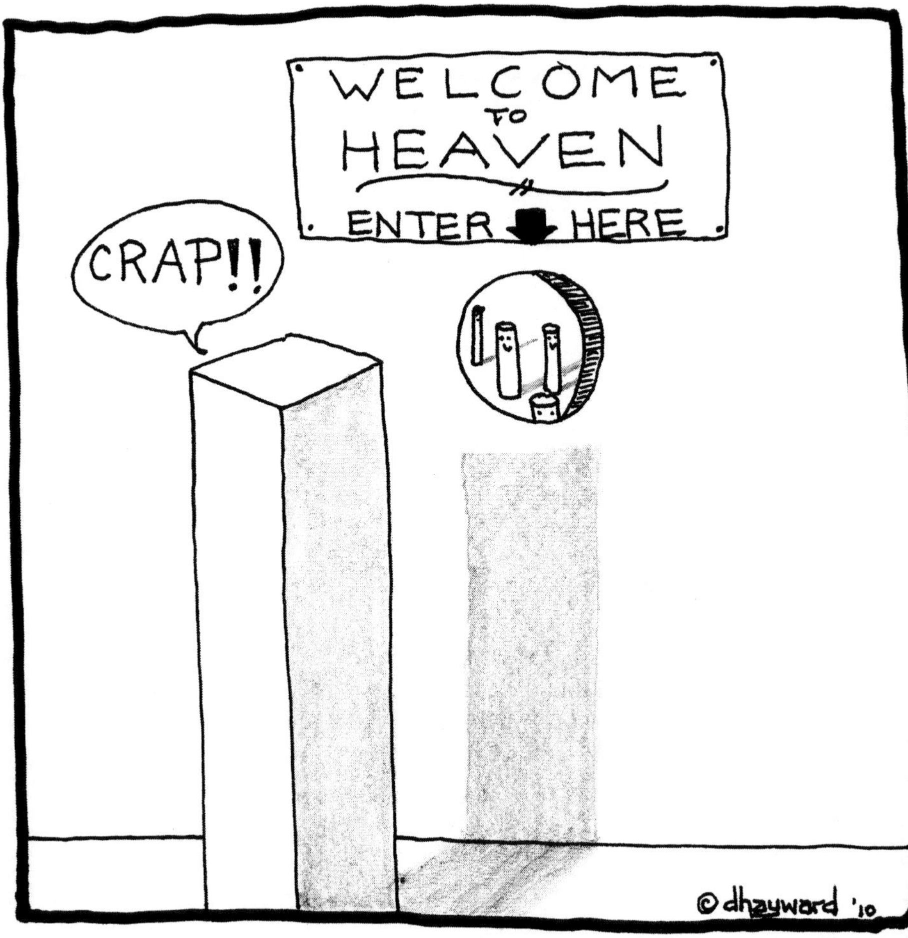
WELCOME TO HEAVEN
ENTER HERE
CRAP!!
© dhayward '10

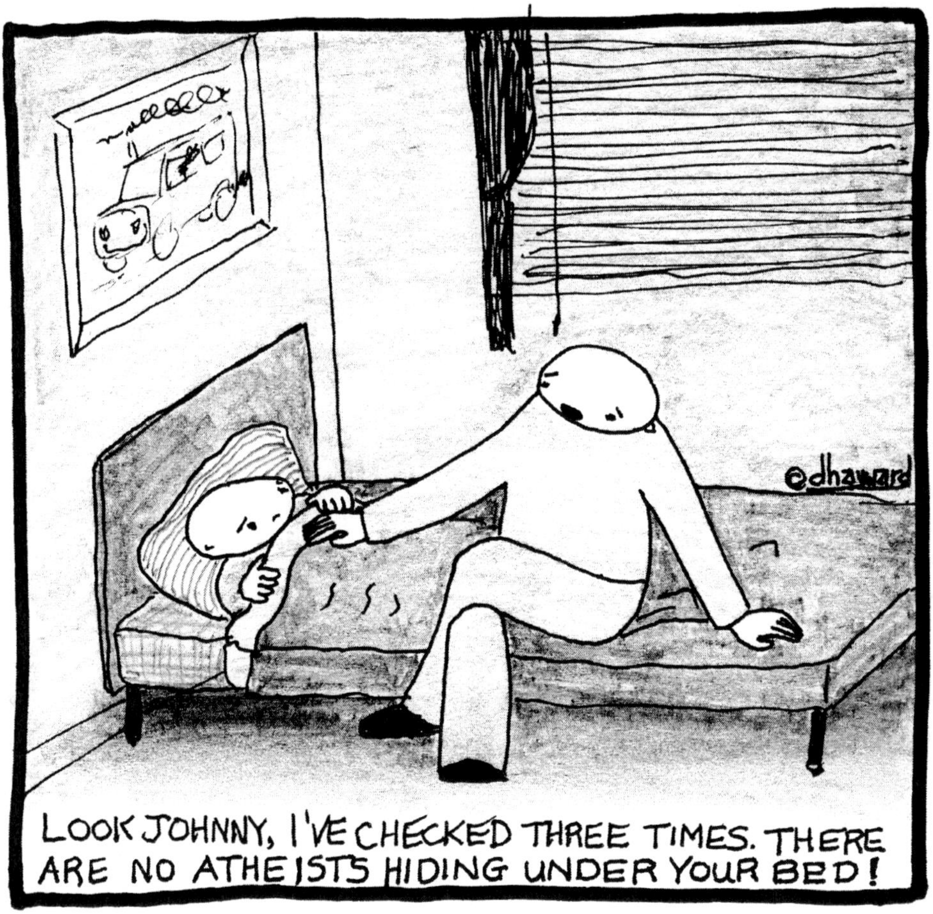
@dhayward
LOOK JOHNNY, I'VE CHECKED THREE TIMES. THERE ARE NO ATHEISTS HIDING UNDER YOUR BED!

The way some people talk about atheists, you'd think they were all monsters. Not all.

012

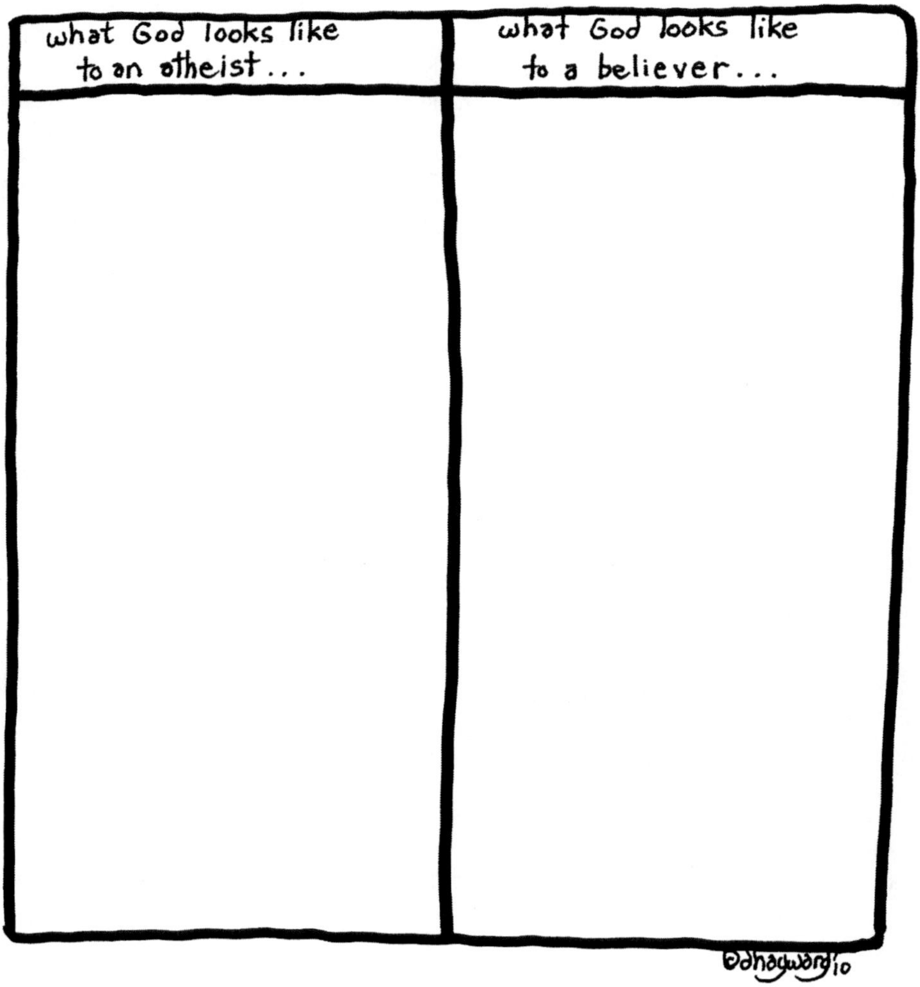
what God looks like to an atheist...
what God looks like to a believer...
©dhayward'10

Funny, but when this first started making its way across the web, people said they were having trouble downloading the image. Then they realized there wasn't one. Perfect!

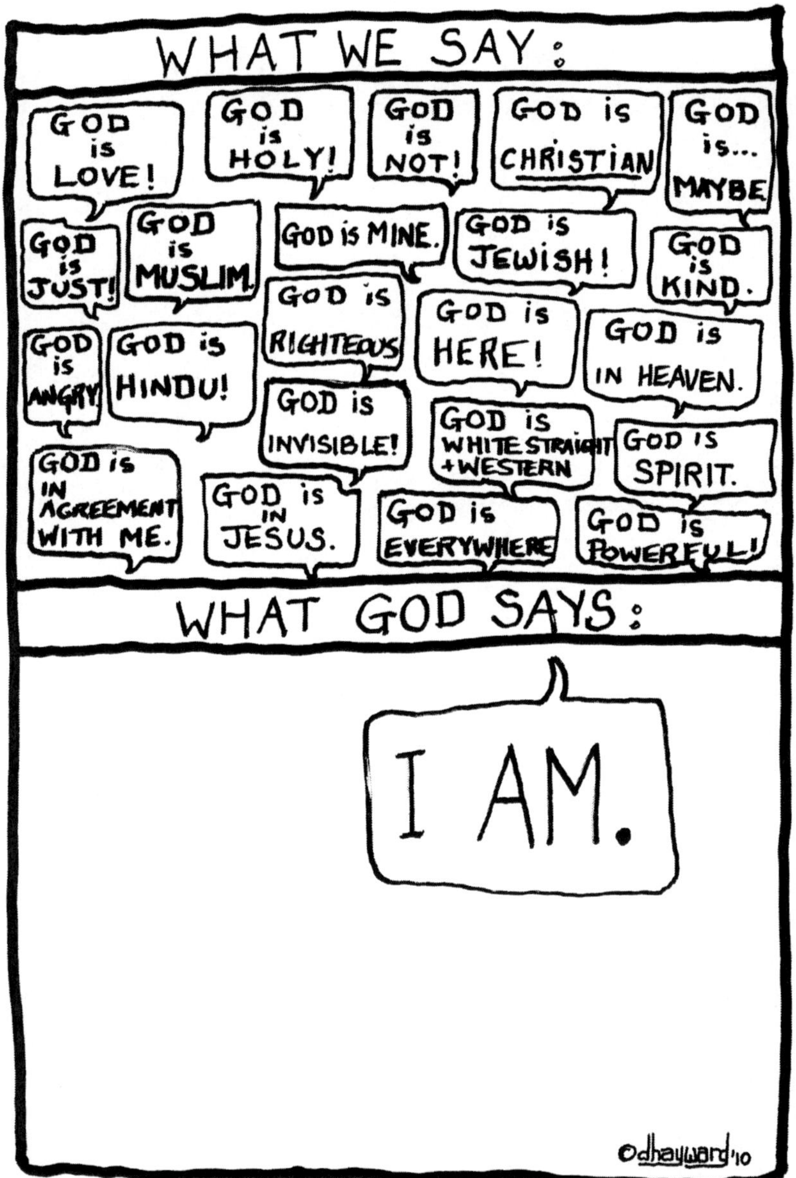
WHAT WE SAY:
GOD is LOVE!
GOD is HOLY!
GOD is NOT!
GOD is CHRISTIAN
GOD is... MAYBE
GOD is JUST!
GOD is MUSLIM.
GOD is MINE.
GOD is JEWISH!
GOD is KIND.
GOD is RIGHTEOUS
GOD is HERE!
GOD is IN HEAVEN.
GOD is ANGRY
GOD is HINDU!
GOD is INVISIBLE!
GOD is WHITE STRAIGHT +WESTERN
GOD IS SPIRIT.
GOD is IN AGREEMENT WITH ME.
GOD is IN JESUS.
GOD is EVERYWHERE
GOD is POWERFUL!
WHAT GOD SAYS:
I AM.
©dhayward'10

Isn't it interesting that in a world where everyone has an opinion of God and everyone has something to say about it, God simply chose to be known as "I Am"? Period.

THE ECUMENICAL CANOE TRIP

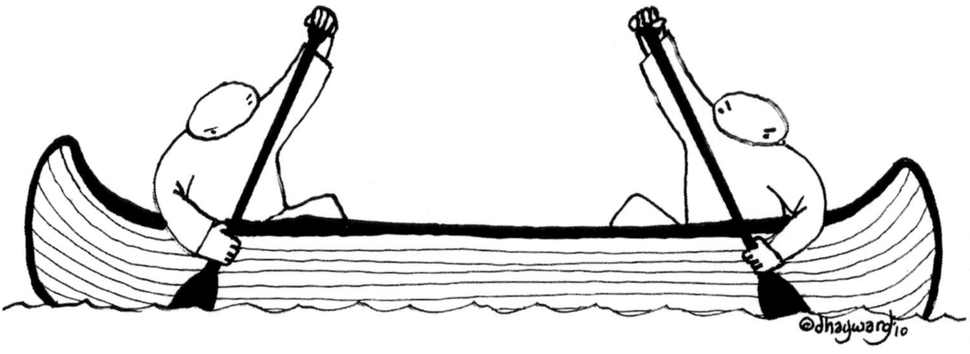
©dhayward'10

The Ecumenical Bike

©dhayward

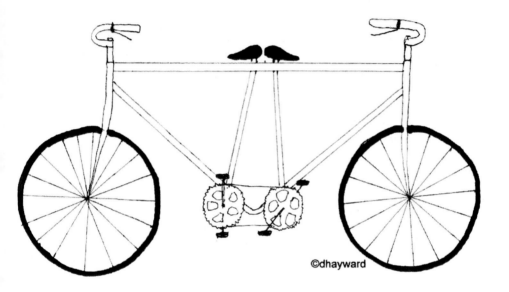

016

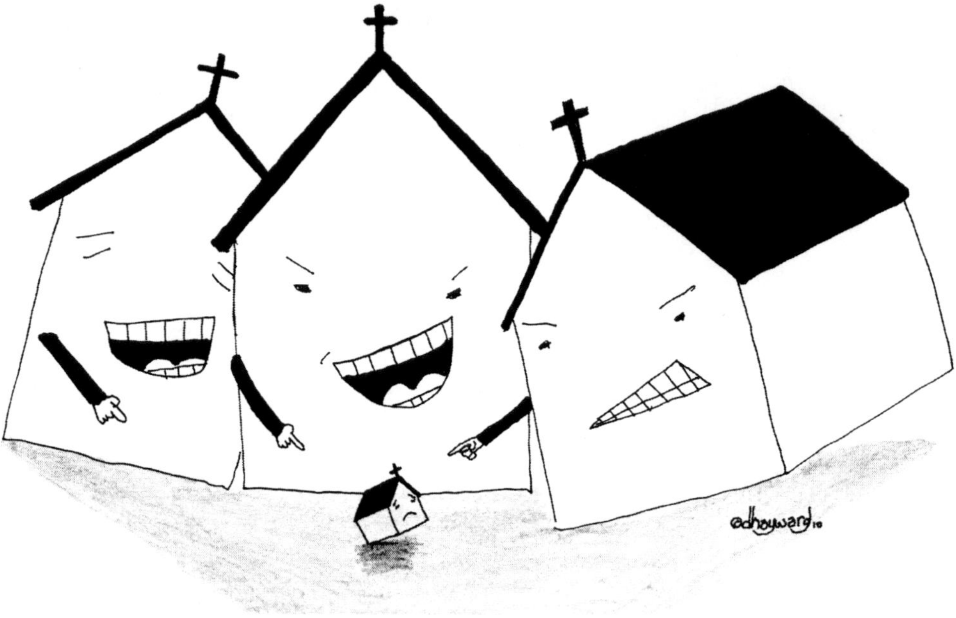
©dhayward10

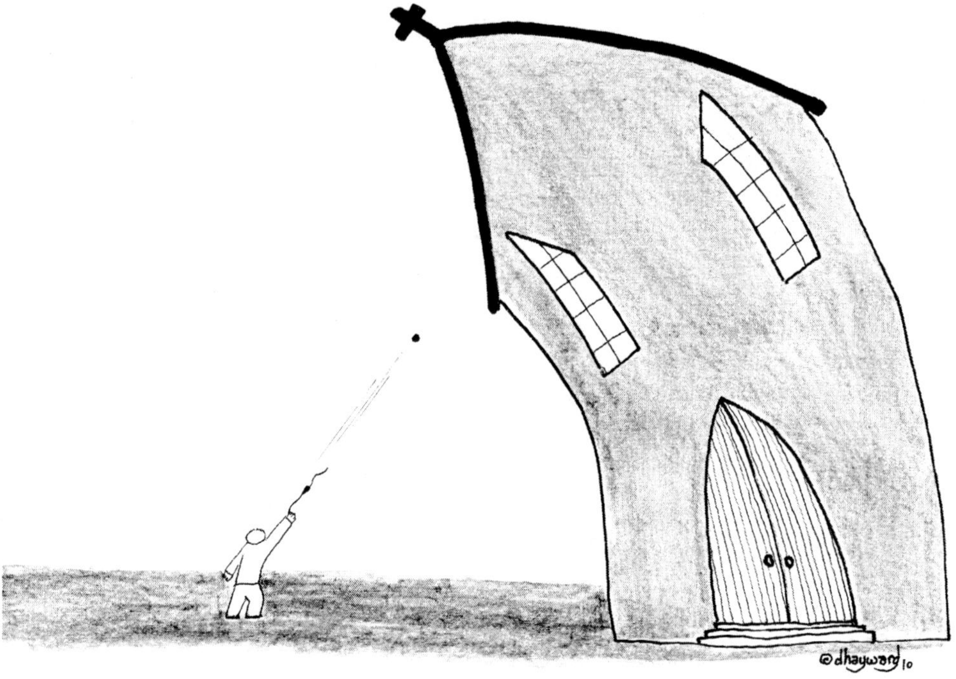
©dhayward10

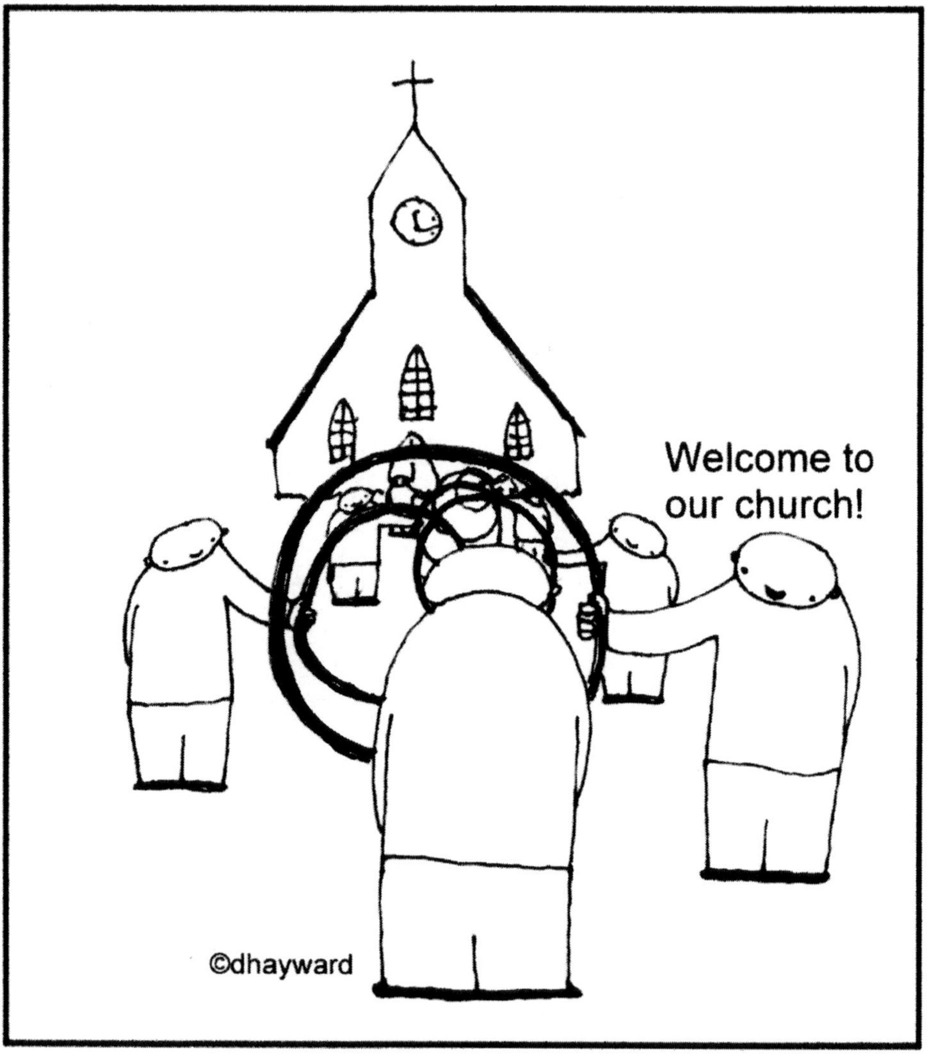
Welcome to
our church!
©dhayward

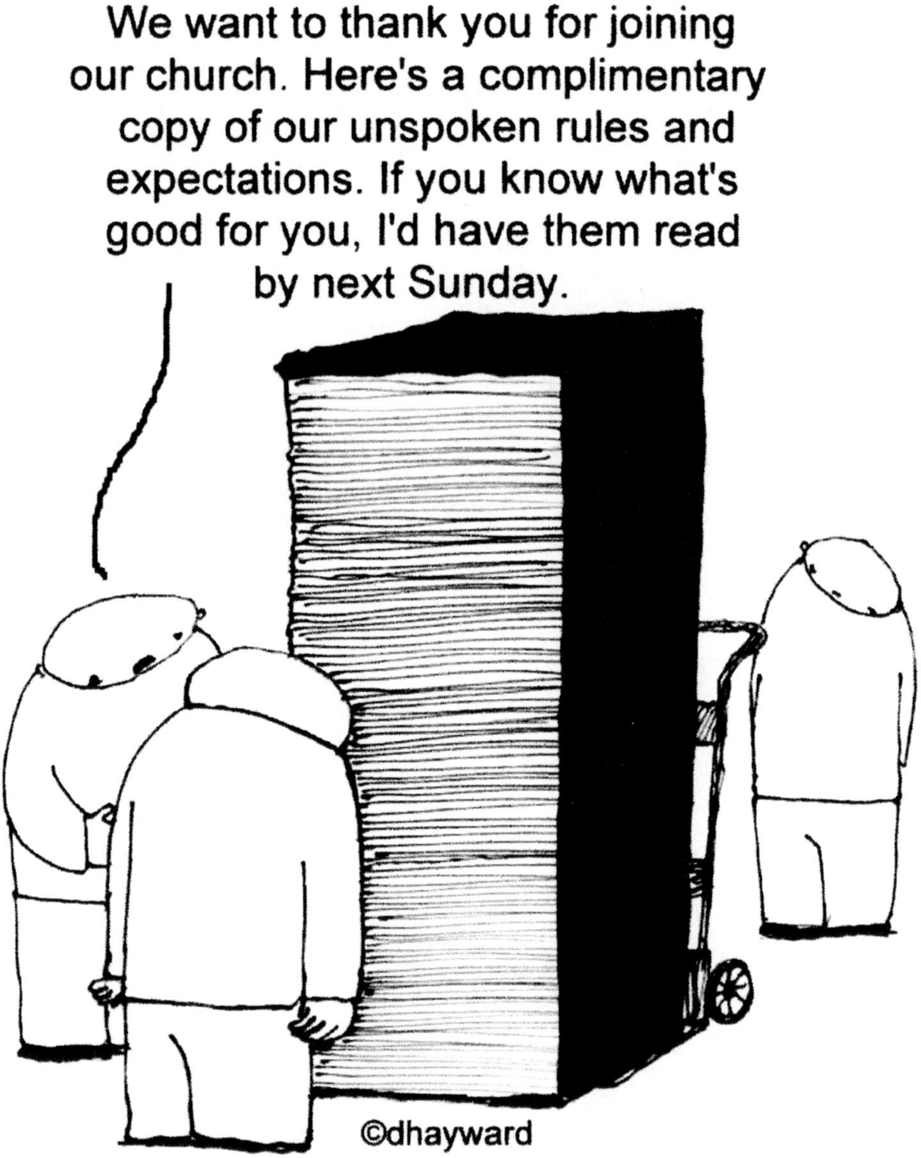
We want to thank you for joining our church. Here's a complimentary copy of our unspoken rules and expectations. If you know what's good for you, I'd have them read by next Sunday.
©dhayward

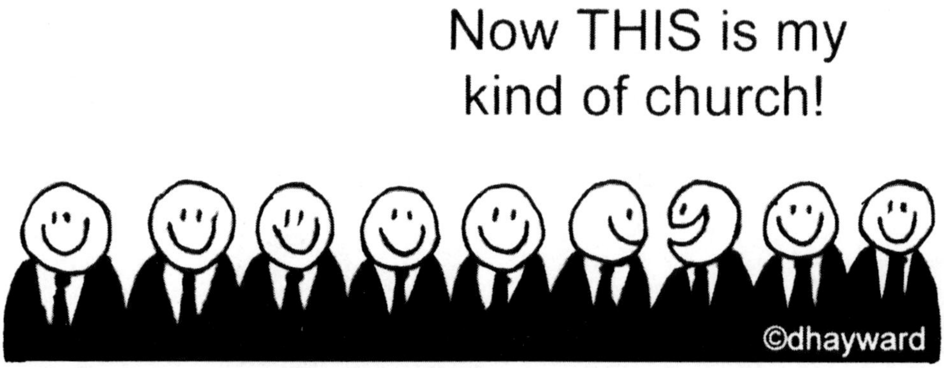
Now THIS is my
kind of church!
©dhayward

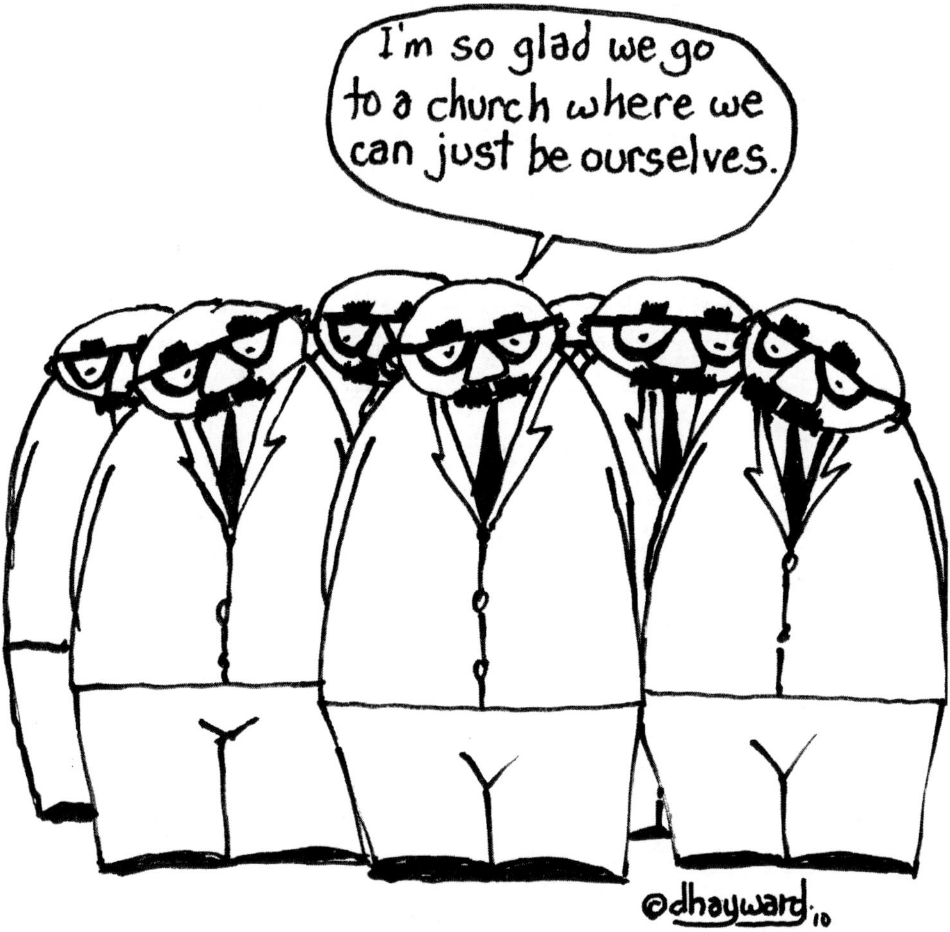
I'm so glad we go to a church where we can just be ourselves.
@dhayward.10

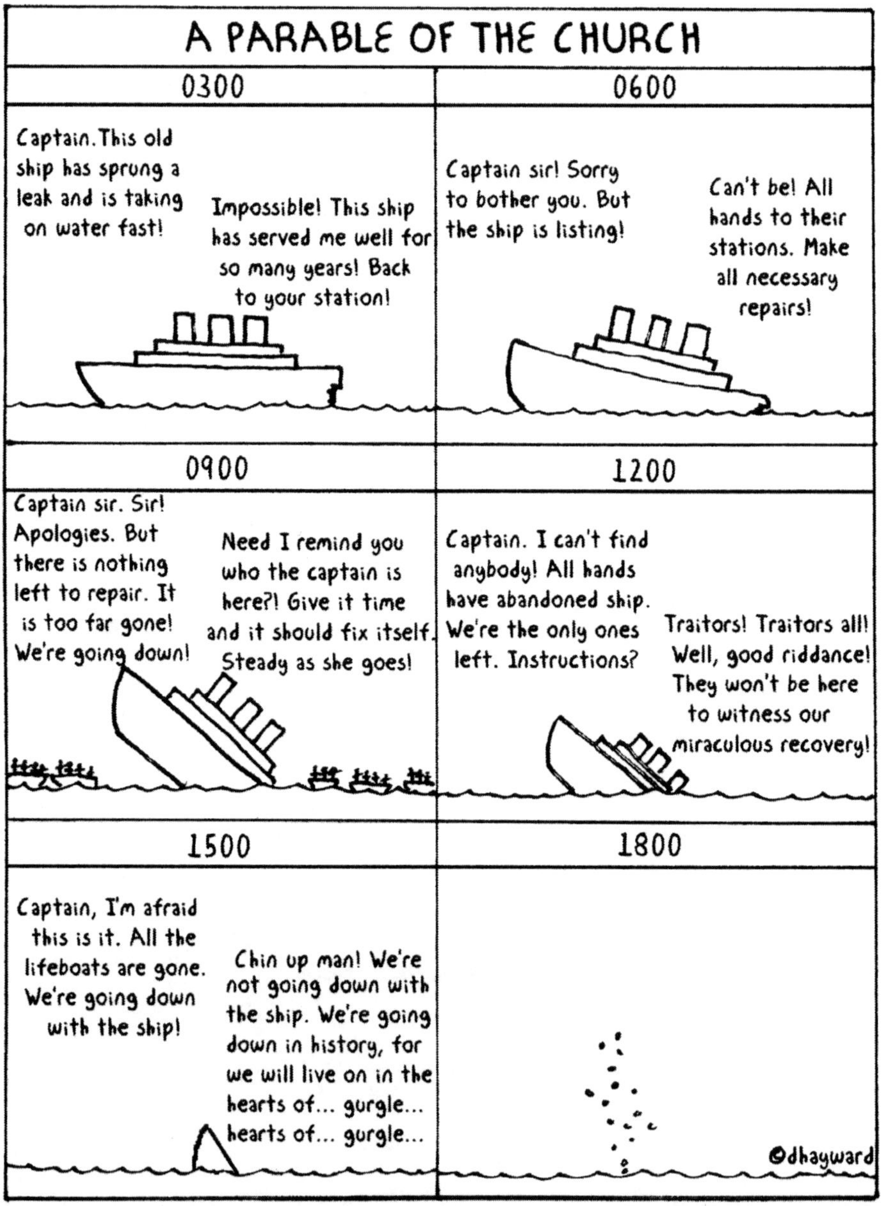
A PARABLE OF THE CHURCH
0300
Captain. This old ship has sprung a leak and is taking on water fast!
Impossible! This ship has served me well for so many years! Back to your station!
0600
Captain sir! Sorry to bother you. But the ship is listing!
Can't be! All hands to their stations. Make all necessary repairs!
0900
Captain sir. Sir! Apologies. But there is nothing left to repair. It is too far gone! We're going down!
Need I remind you who the captain is here?! Give it time and it should fix itself. Steady as she goes!
1200
Captain. I can't find anybody! All hands have abandoned ship. We're the only ones left. Instructions?
Traitors! Traitors all! Well, good riddance! They won't be here to witness our miraculous recovery!
1500
Captain, I'm afraid this is it. All the lifeboats are gone. We're going down with the ship!
Chin up man! We're not going down with the ship. We're going down in history, for we will live on in the hearts of... gurgle... hearts of... gurgle...
1800
©dhayward

When I posted this cartoon on my blog, someone asked if the numbers were military hours (as I intended), or if they were the years. It surprised me how both could work.

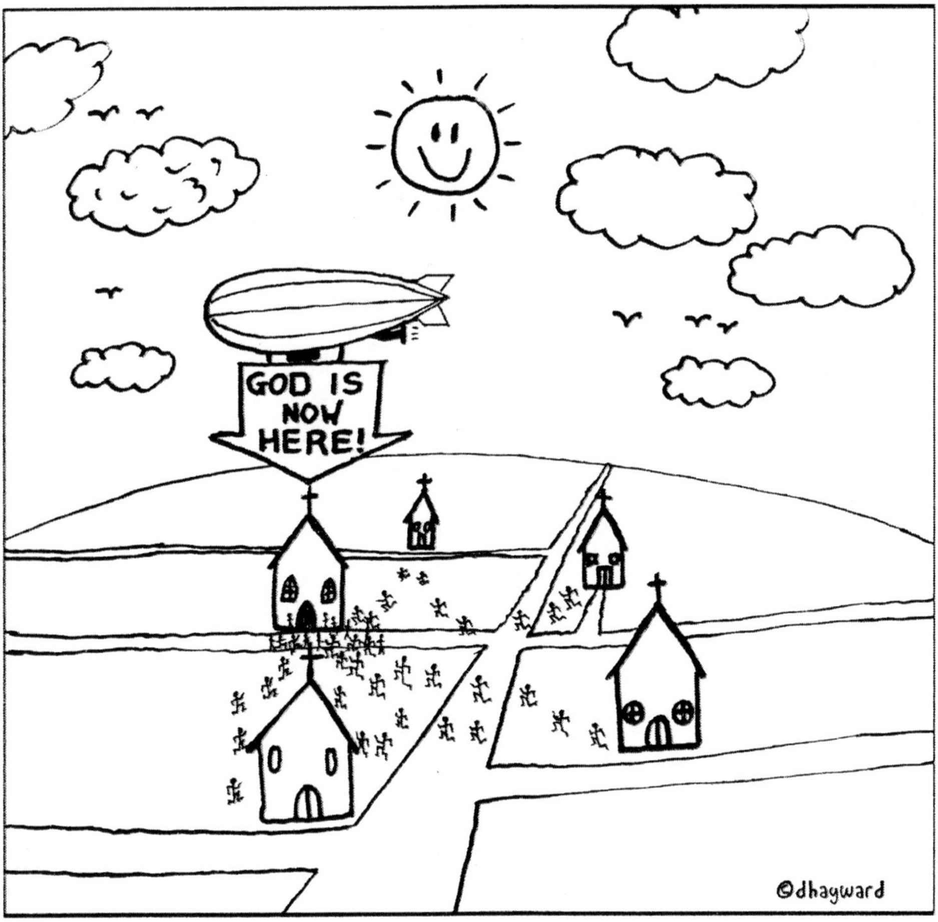
GOD IS NOW HERE!
©dhayward

I live in a small city. If something exciting is happening at one church, there's a transfer of people. Word gets around. So do people.

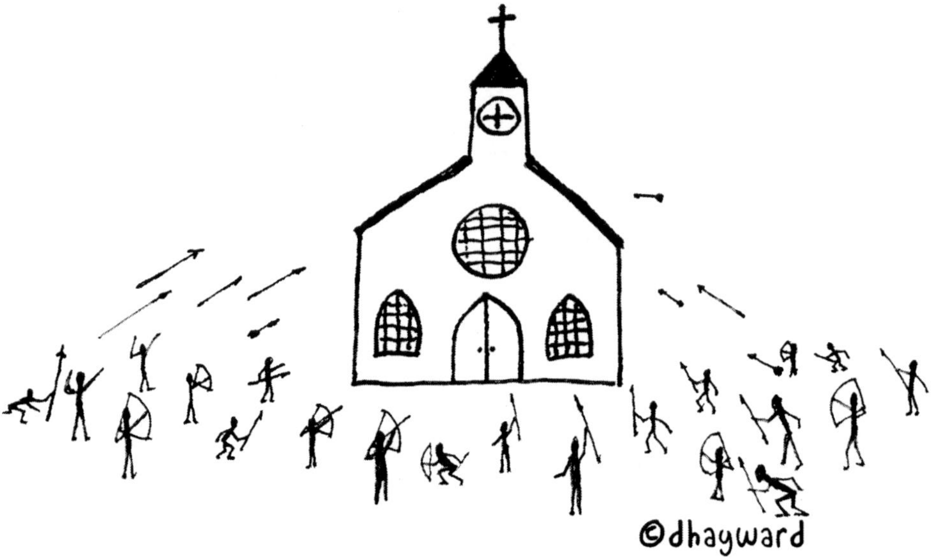
©dhayward

I couldn't believe the reaction this cartoon provoked on my blog. It started a rather heated dialog about Muslims attacking the church. What?

025

Okay people, I commend your courage. What you are about to do is dangerous. I can guarantee that you will all be wounded, and some of you will not come out of there alive. So, if you're ready, let's go! And watch your back!
©dhayward '10

026

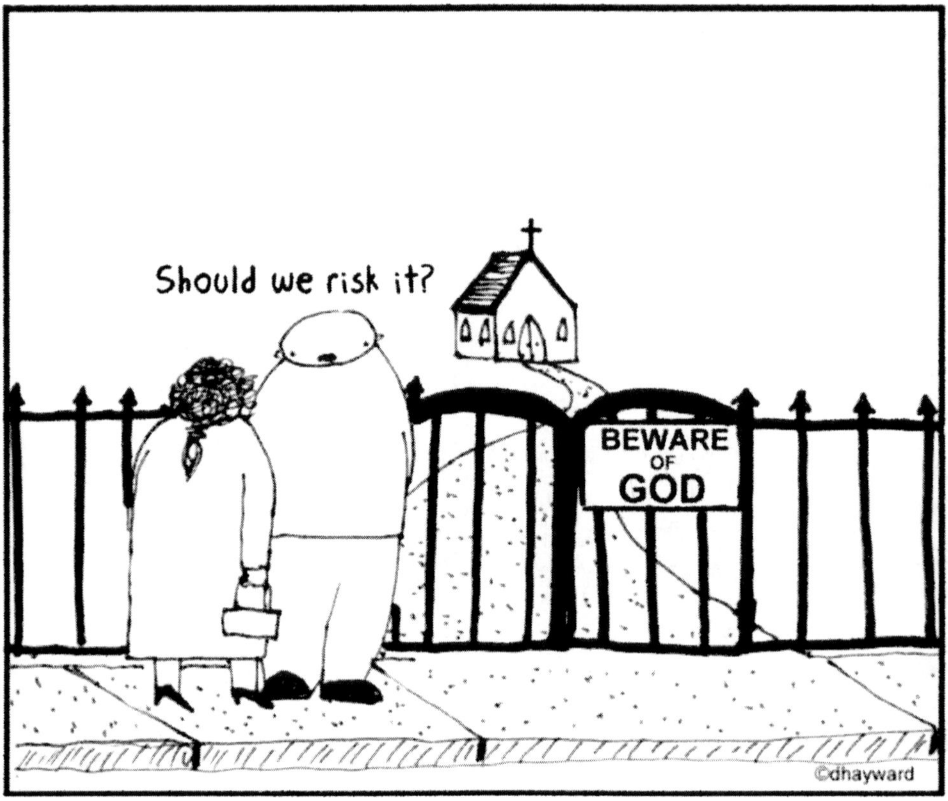
Should we risk it?
BEWARE
OF
GOD
©dhayward

Annie Dillard, in her book, Teaching a Stone to Talk, writes, "On the whole, I do not find Christians, outside of the catacombs, sufficiently sensible of conditions. Does anyone have the foggiest idea what sort of power we so blithely invoke? Or, as I suspect, does no one believe a word of it? The churches are children playing on the floor with their chemistry sets, mixing up a batch of TNT to kill a Sunday morning. It is madness to wear ladies' straw hats and velvet hats to church; we should all be wearing crash helmets. Ushers should issue life preservers and signal flares; they should lash us to our pews. For the sleeping god may wake someday and take offense, or the waking god may draw us out to where we can never return."

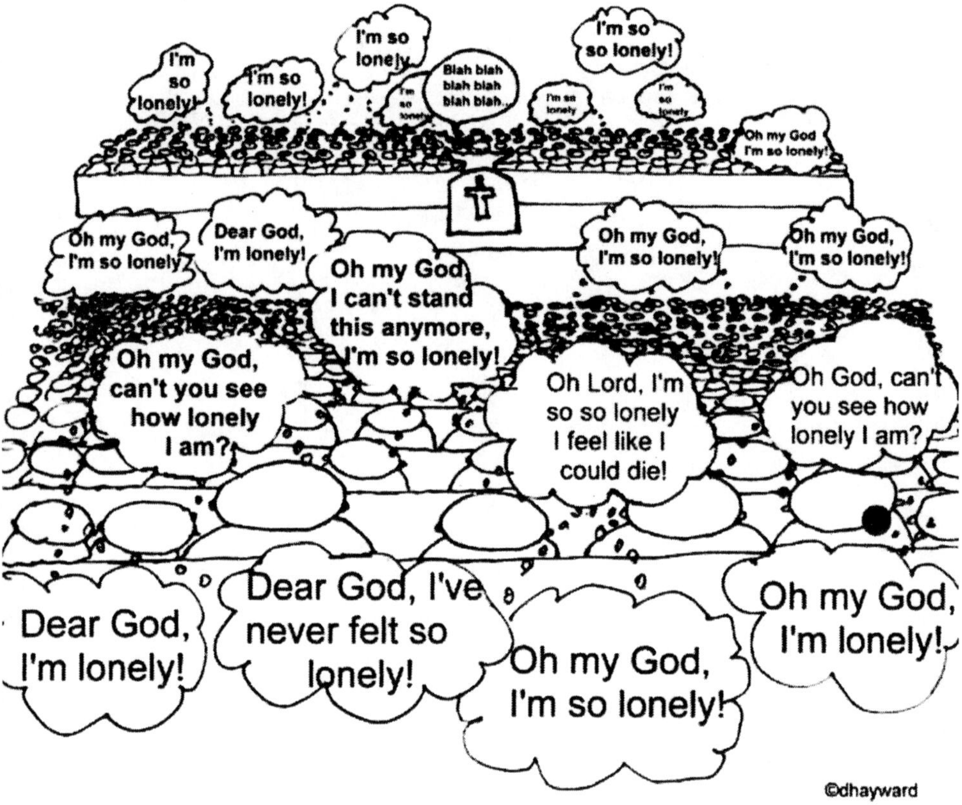
I'm so lonely!
I'm so lonely!
I'm so lonely
Blah blah blah blah blah blah...
I'm so lonely
I'm so lonely!
I'm so lonely
Oh my God I'm so lonely!
Oh my God, I'm so lonely
Dear God, I'm lonely!
Oh my God I can't stand this anymore, I'm so lonely!
Oh my God, I'm so lonely!
Oh my God, I'm so lonely!
Oh my God, can't you see how lonely I am?
Oh Lord, I'm so so lonely I feel like I could die!
Oh God, can't you see how lonely I am?
Dear God, I'm lonely!
Dear God, I've never felt so lonely!
Oh my God, I'm so lonely!
Oh my God, I'm lonely!
©dhayward

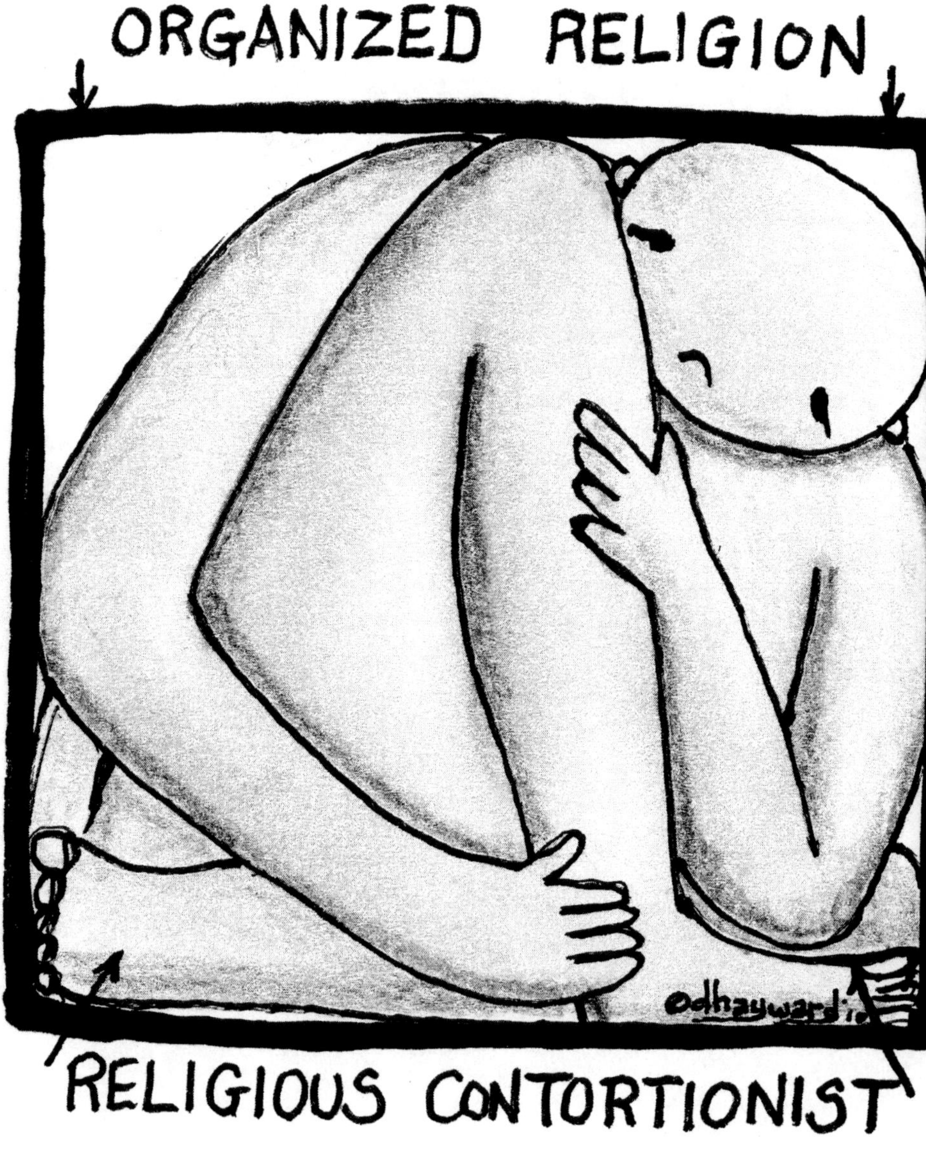
ORGANIZED RELIGION
RELIGIOUS CONTORTIONIST
©dhayward

The Pastor's Dream

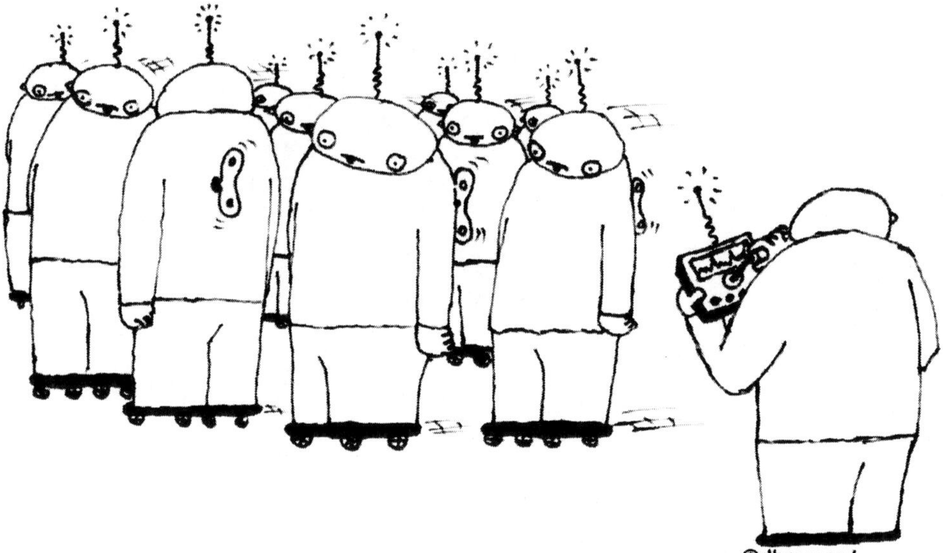
©dhavward

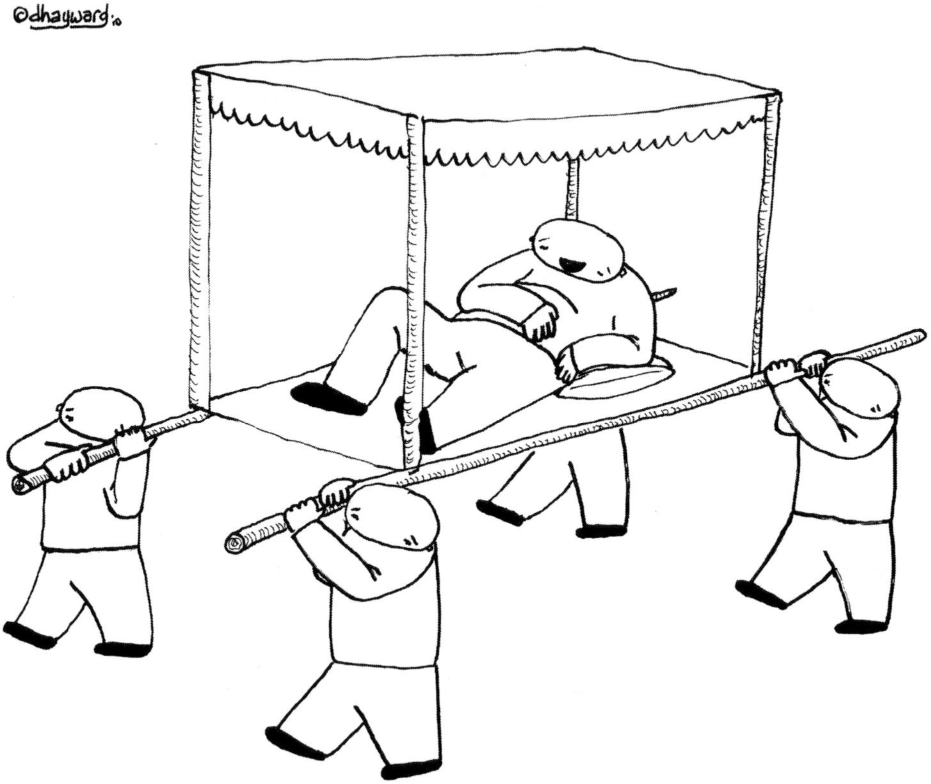
©dhayward'10

" Just remember guys: you are doing this for God, not for me!"

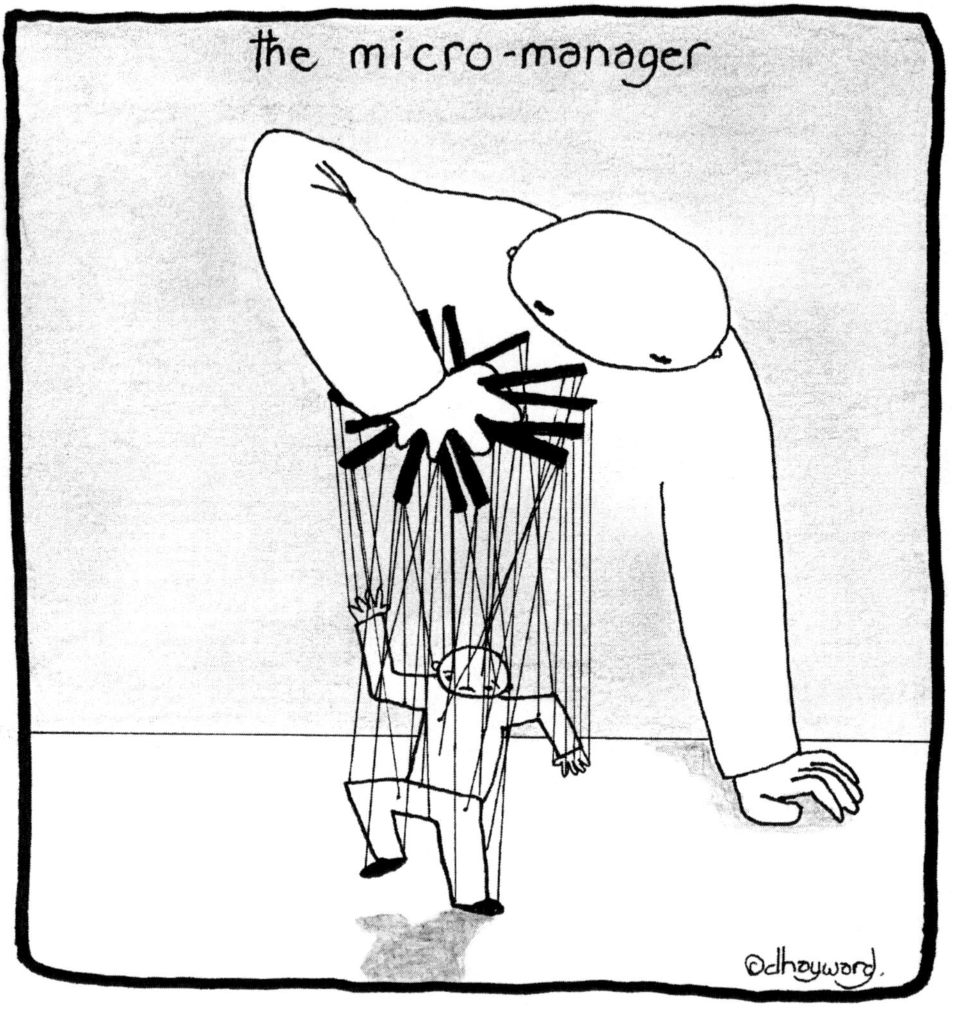
the micro-manager
©dhayward.

032

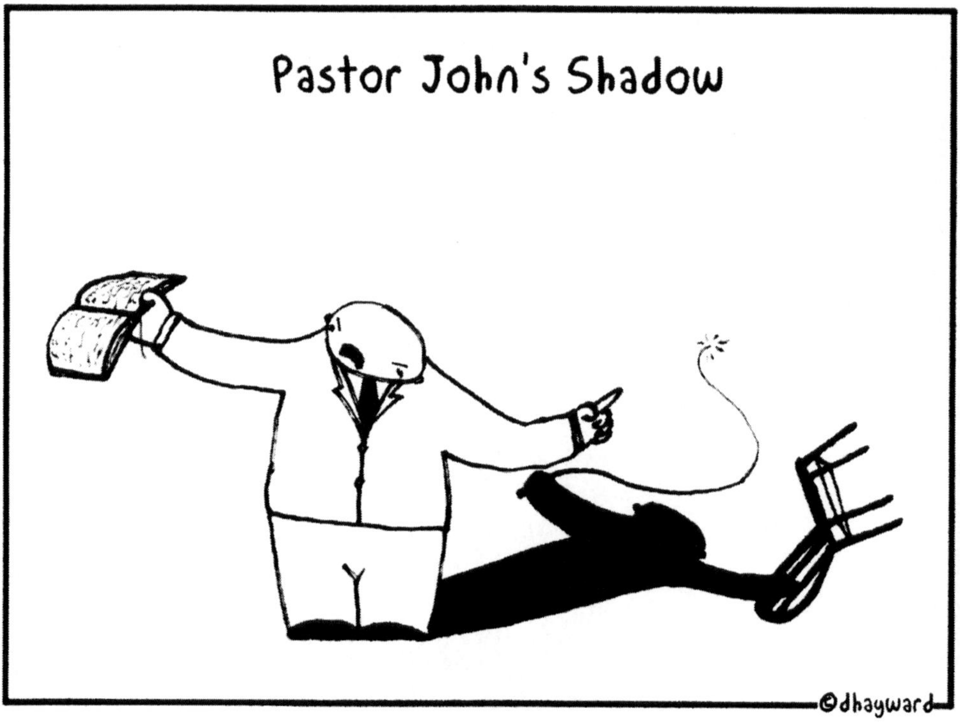
Pastor John's Shadow
©dhayward

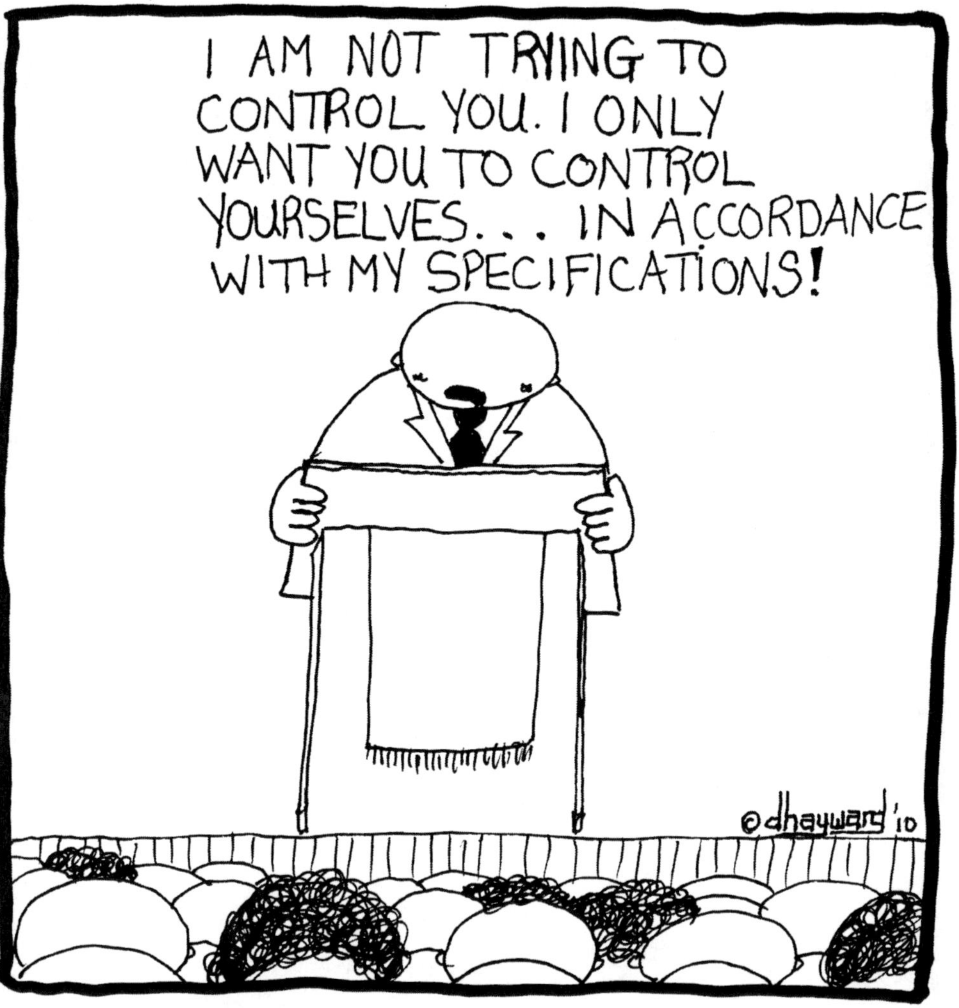
I AM NOT TRYING TO CONTROL YOU. I ONLY WANT YOU TO CONTROL YOURSELVES... IN ACCORDANCE WITH MY SPECIFICATIONS!
©dhayward '10

No one ever says that they want to completely control you. However, if you aren't too damaged, you definitely know when the powers of control, coercion and manipulation are at work. It's like saying, "I didn't shoot you. My gun did!"

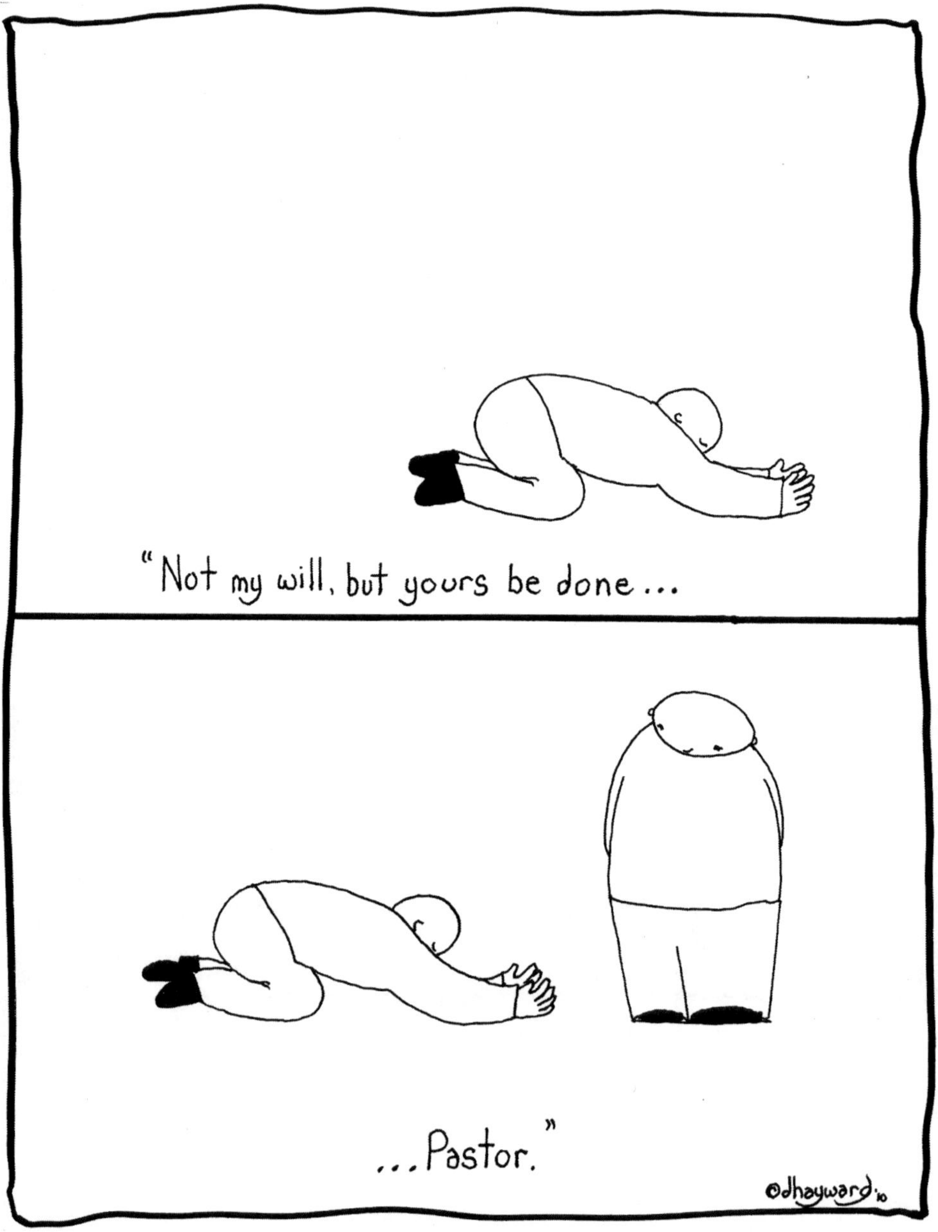
"Not my will, but yours be done...
...Pastor."
©dhayward.10

I've been in this posture. Actually, both. Ugly and inadmissible.

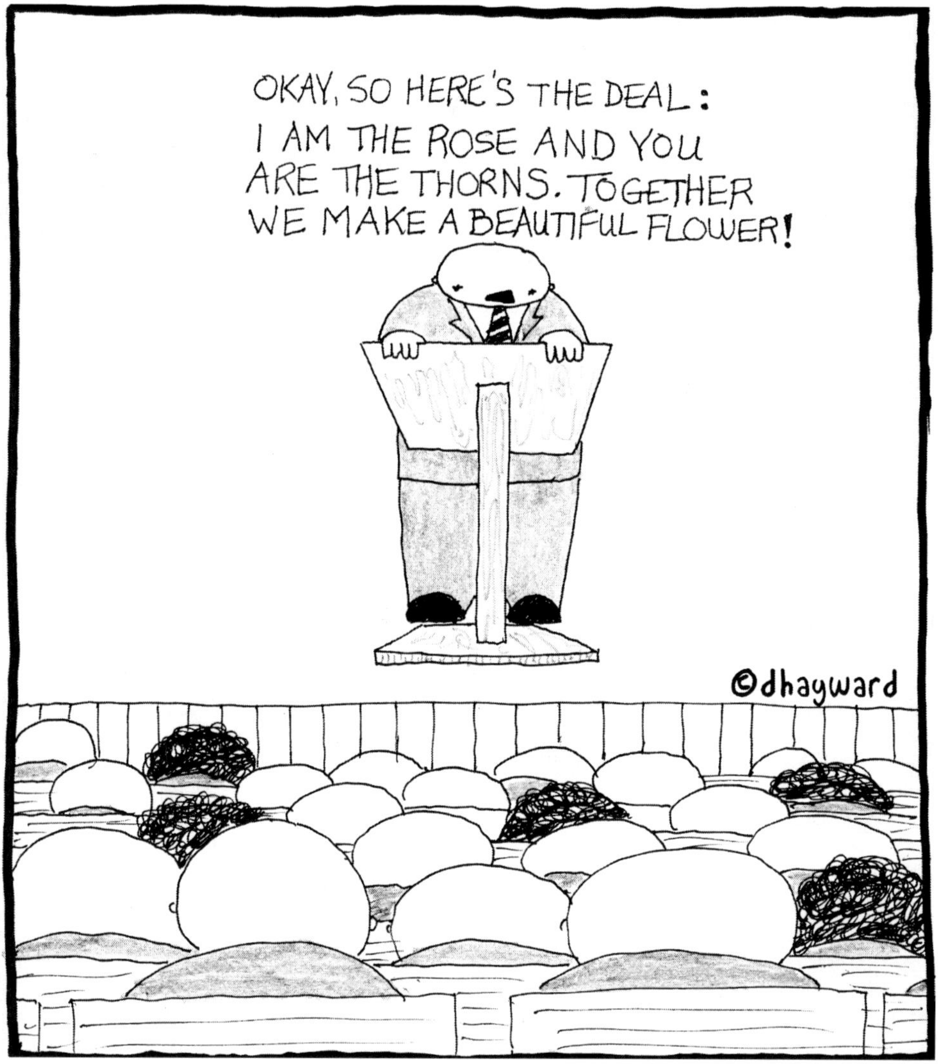
OKAY, SO HERE'S THE DEAL:
I AM THE ROSE AND YOU ARE THE THORNS. TOGETHER WE MAKE A BEAUTIFUL FLOWER!
©dhayward

The temptation for leaders to feel entitled is sometimes impossible to resist.

nakedpastor101
036

"Lord, I thank you that I have such a peaceful church."

Gag orders. Have you ever been in a situation where you are invited to speak your mind, but you know when you do you're going to get in trouble?

"I just felt I needed to come straight to you and say that I find that your leadership is just a little too controlling for me. I am an adult, and expect to be treated like ...
©dhayward10

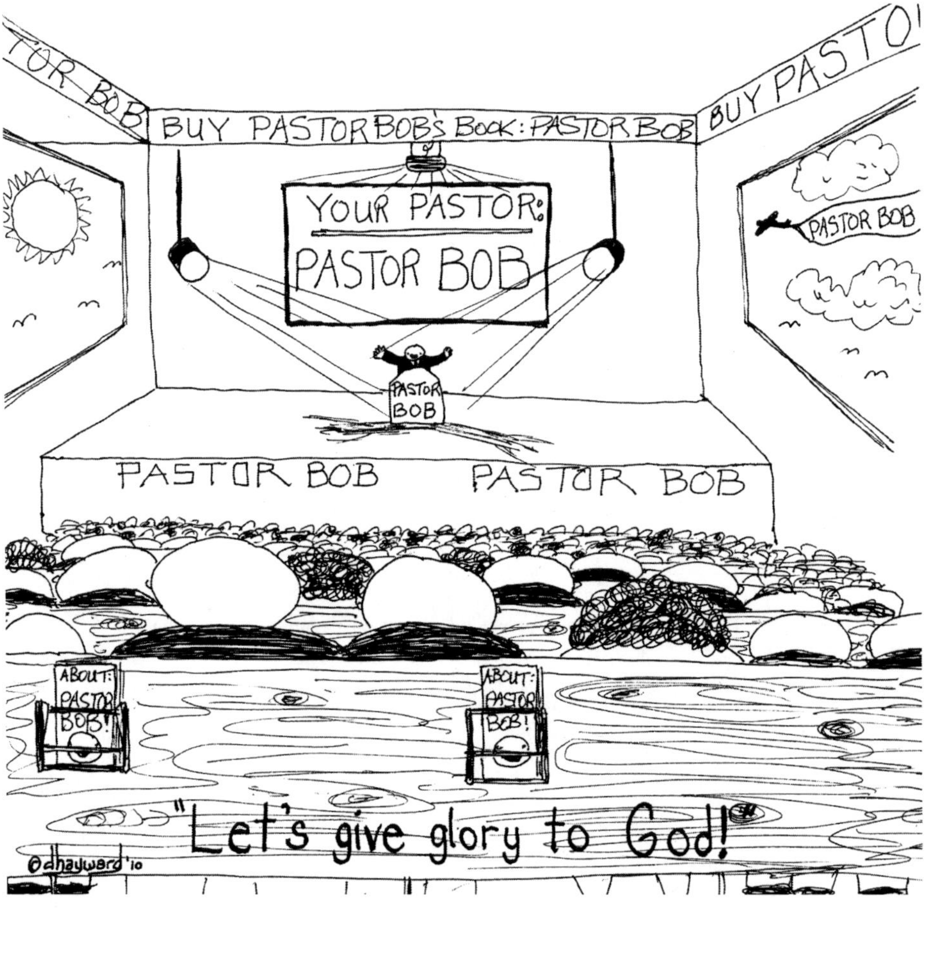
BUY PASTOR BOB'S BOOK: PASTOR BOB
BUY PASTO
TOR BOB
YOUR PASTOR:
PASTOR BOB
PASTOR BOB
PASTOR
BOB
PASTOR BOB PASTOR BOB
ABOUT: PASTOR BOB!
ABOUT: PASTOR BOB!
"Let's give glory to God!"
©dhayward '10

Pastor, what's our policy on abuse?
Well, we only do spiritual and some emotional, but we try to avoid physical and sexual.
©dhayward

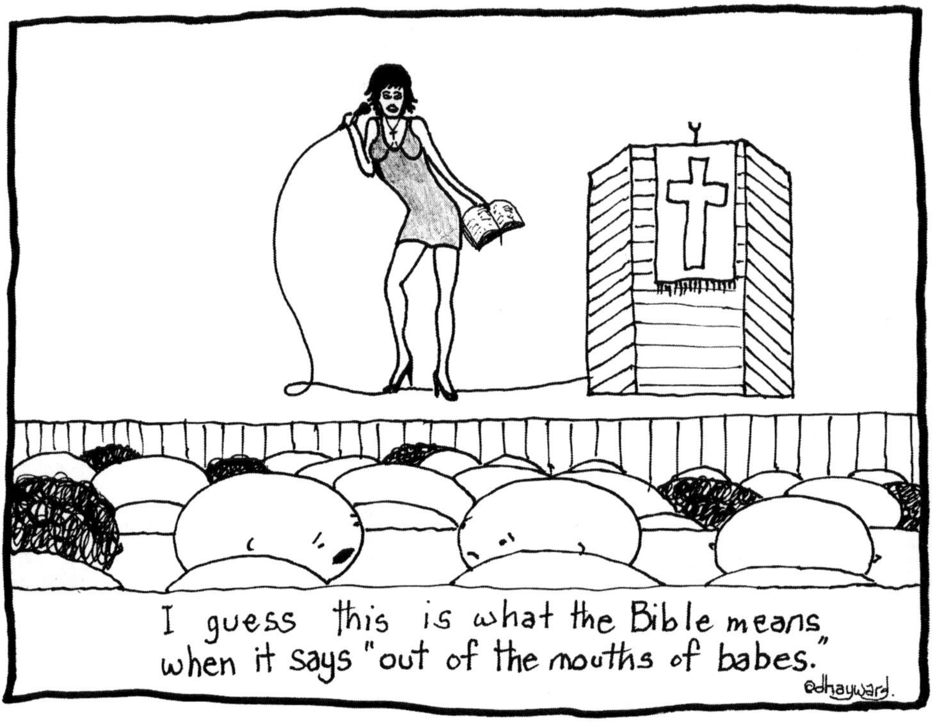
I guess this is what the Bible means when it says "out of the mouths of babes."
©dhayward.

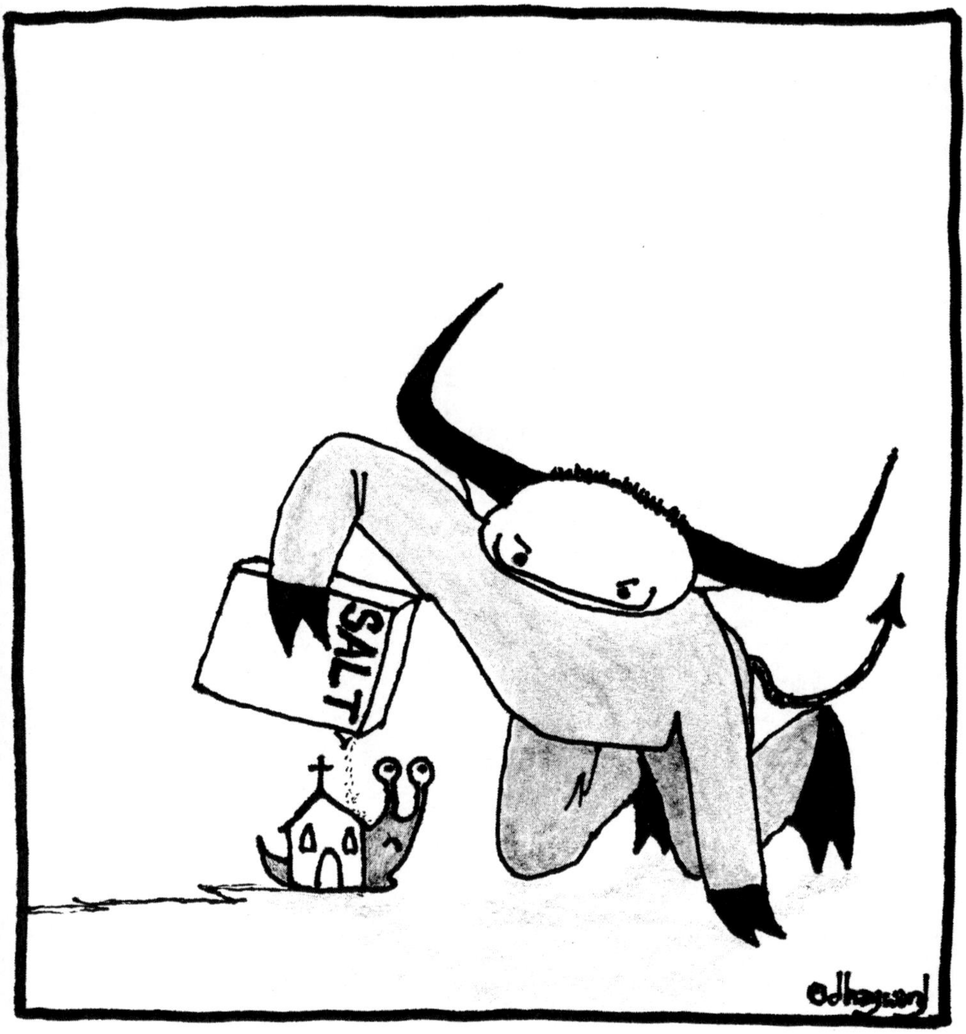
SALT
©dhayward

042

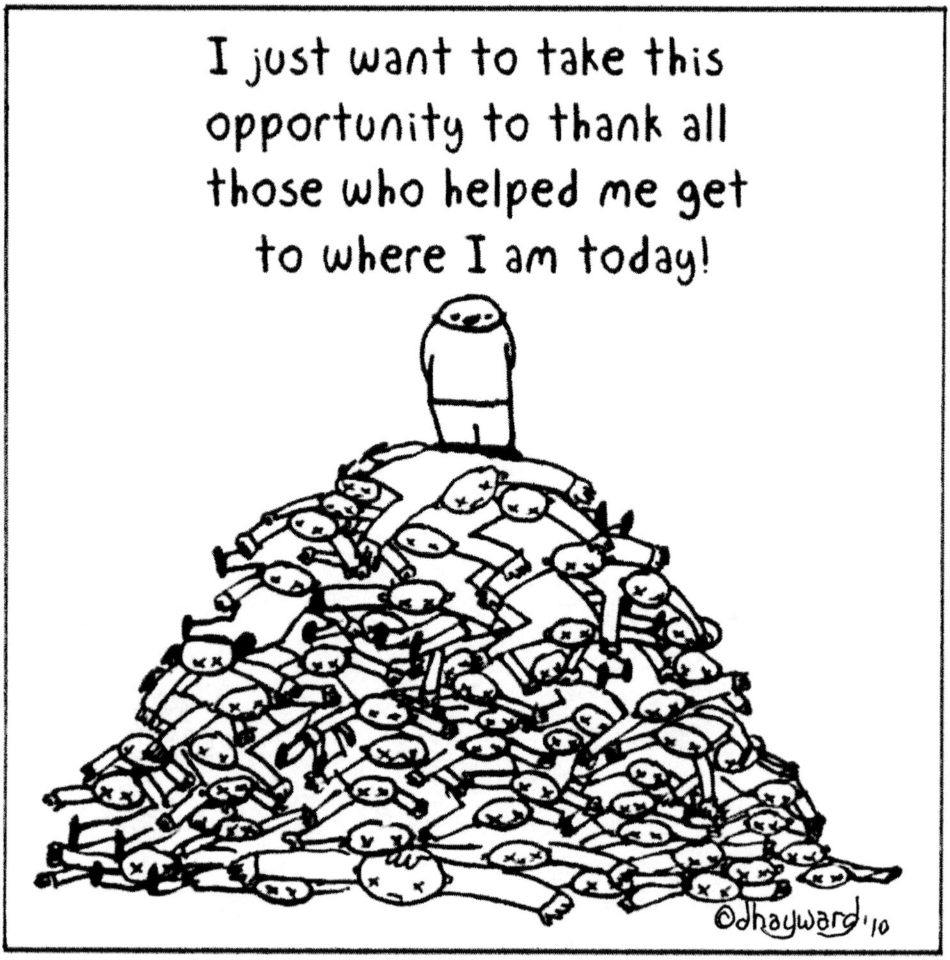
I just want to take this opportunity to thank all those who helped me get to where I am today!
©dhayward '10

Some people have no idea the damage they've caused and the devastation they've personally and indirectly delivered to people.

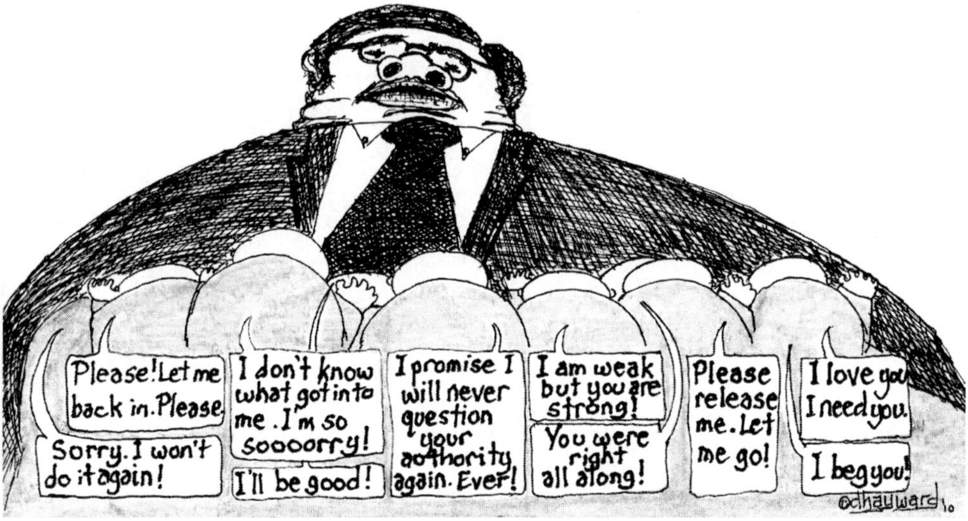
Please! Let me back in. Please.
Sorry. I won't do it again!
I don't know what got into me. I'm so sooooorry!
I'll be good!
I promise I will never question your authority again. Ever!
I am weak but you are strong!
You were right all along!
Please release me. Let me go!
I love you. I need you.
I beg you!
©dhayward 10

I've actually seen this. In real life. Honest.

044

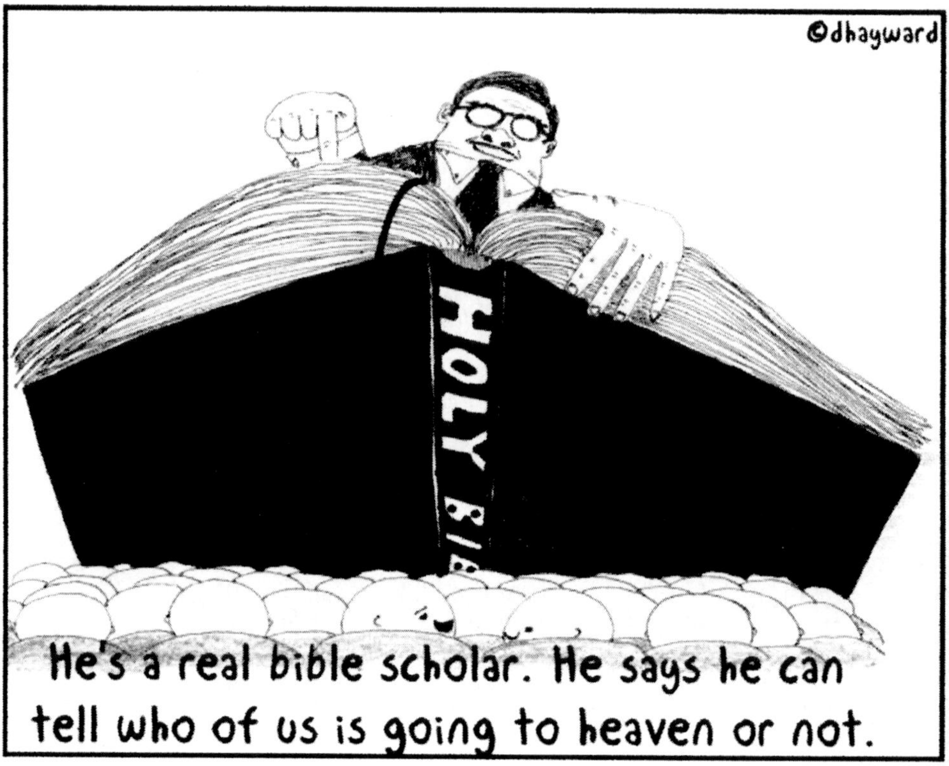
©dhayward
HOLY BIB
He's a real bible scholar. He says he can tell who of us is going to heaven or not.

If we believe the bible is a magical book of spiritual formulas, then the decipherers have all the power.

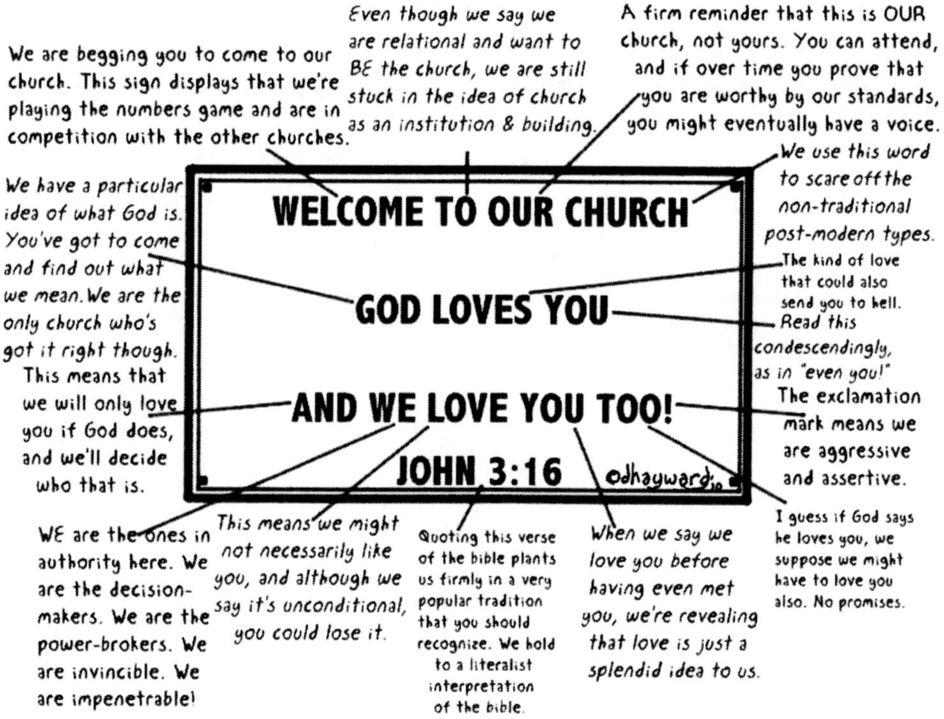
Even though we say we are relational and want to BE the church, we are still stuck in the idea of church as an institution & building.
A firm reminder that this is OUR church, not yours. You can attend, and if over time you prove that you are worthy by our standards, you might eventually have a voice.
We are begging you to come to our church. This sign displays that we're playing the numbers game and are in competition with the other churches.
We use this word to scare off the non-traditional post-modern types.
We have a particular idea of what God is. You've got to come and find out what we mean. We are the only church who's got it right though.
WELCOME TO OUR CHURCH
GOD LOVES YOU
AND WE LOVE YOU TOO!
JOHN 3:16
odhayward10
The kind of love that could also send you to hell.
Read this condescendingly, as in "even you!"
This means that we will only love you if God does, and we'll decide who that is.
The exclamation mark means we are aggressive and assertive.
WE are the ones in authority here. We are the decision-makers. We are the power-brokers. We are invincible. We are impenetrable!
This means we might not necessarily like you, and although we say it's unconditional, you could lose it.
Quoting this verse of the bible plants us firmly in a very popular tradition that you should recognize. We hold to a literalist interpretation of the bible.
When we say we love you before having even met you, we're revealing that love is just a splendid idea to us.
I guess if God says he loves you, we suppose we might have to love you also. No promises.

I had been reading a lot of the deconstructionists. I especially appreciate Derrida. So I thought I would have a little bit of fun deconstructing a church sign. A friend of mine, later in the day, sent me a copy of an article from a newspaper where someone had deconstructed the obituary of Derrida. Beautiful!

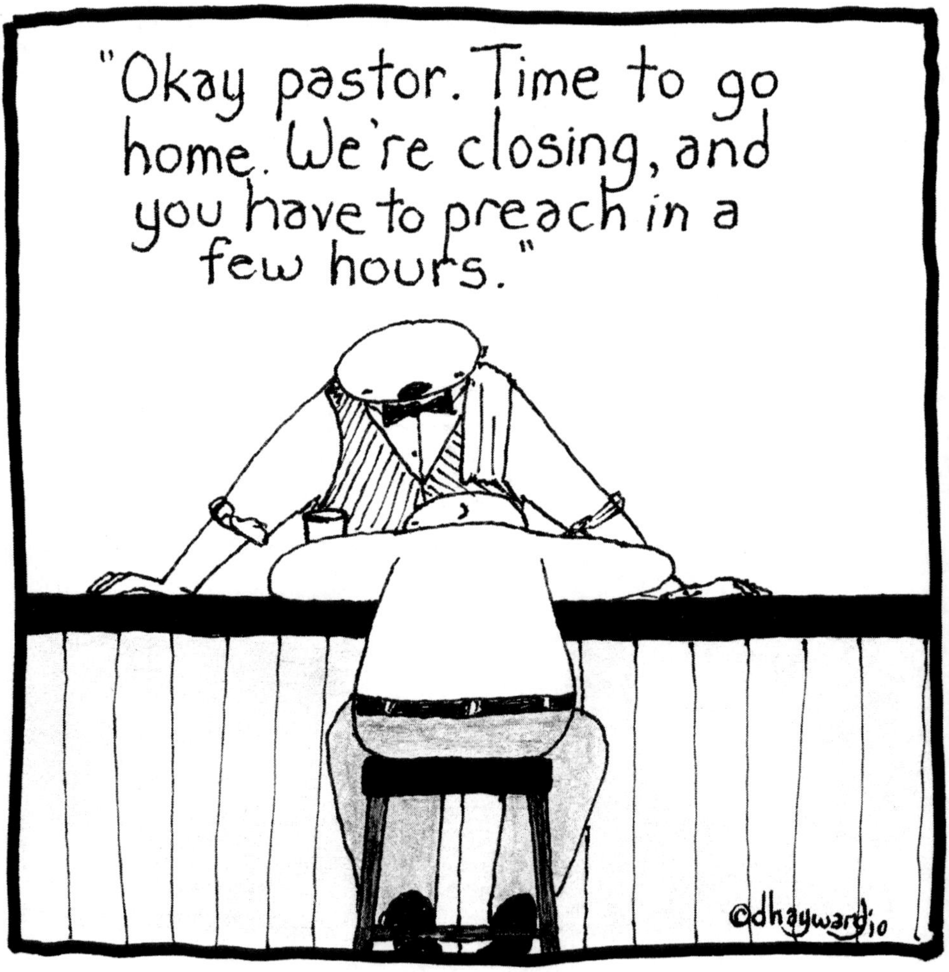
"Okay pastor. Time to go home. We're closing, and you have to preach in a few hours."
©dhayward'10

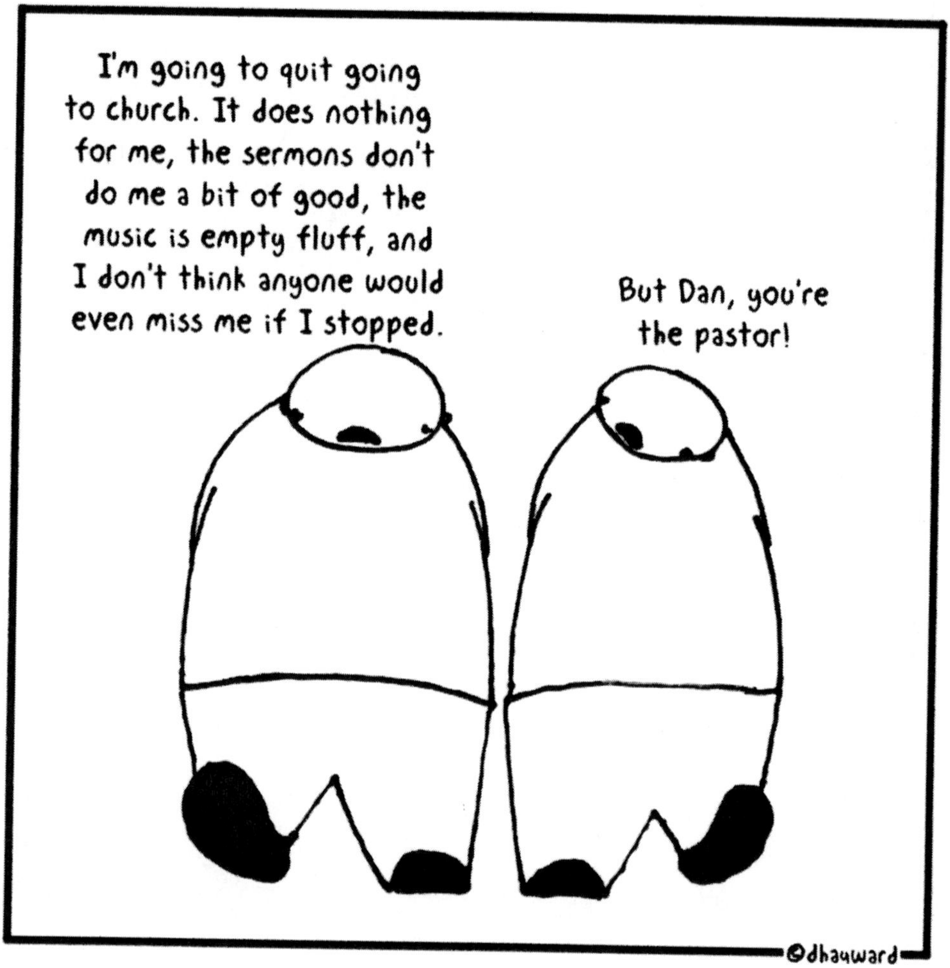
I'm going to quit going to church. It does nothing for me, the sermons don't do me a bit of good, the music is empty fluff, and I don't think anyone would even miss me if I stopped.
But Dan, you're the pastor!
©dhayward

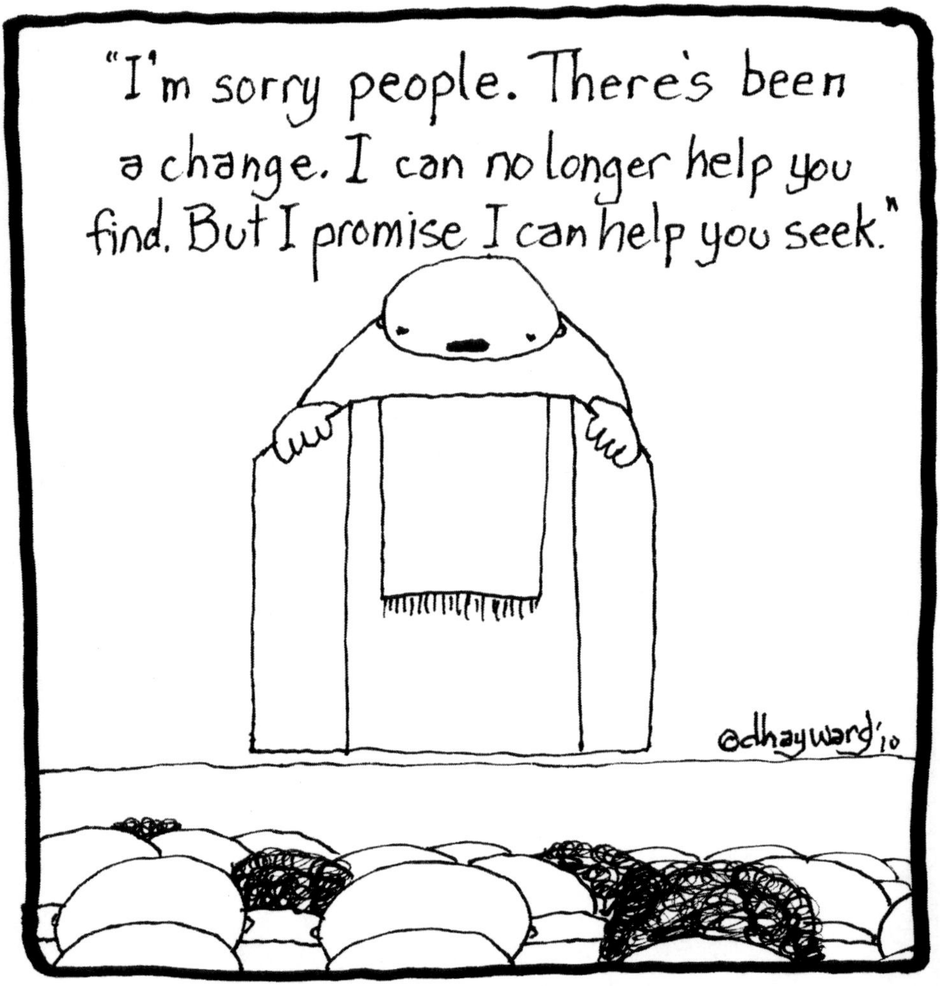
"I'm sorry people. There's been a change. I can no longer help you find. But I promise I can help you seek."
©dhayward'10

When I drew this cartoon I was thinking of Henri Nouwen, the Wounded Healer himself, in the tradition of Jesus. Many others noted the connection too.

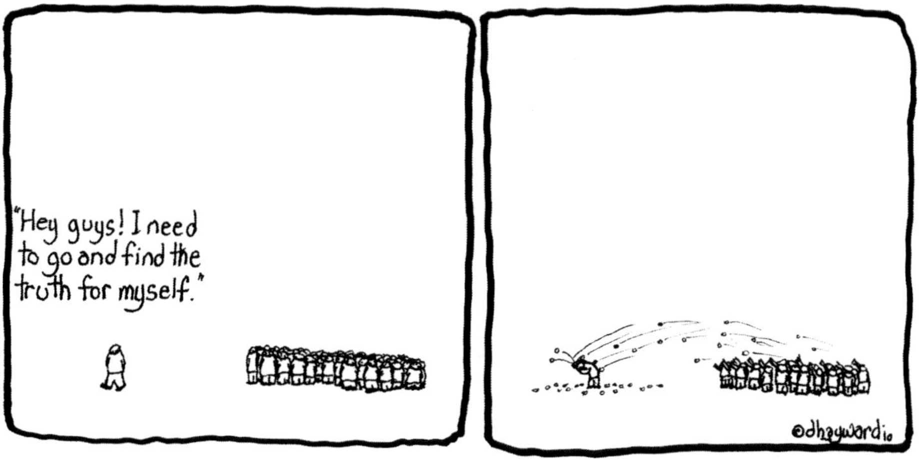
"Hey guys! I need to go and find the truth for myself."
©dhayward10

The great American essayist Wendell Berry wrote of America in Citizenship Papers, "An inescapable requirement of true patriotism, love for one's land, is a vigilant distrust of any determinative power, elected or unelected, that may preside over it." The same applies to the church. But it's a risky endeavor, as this guy found out.

050

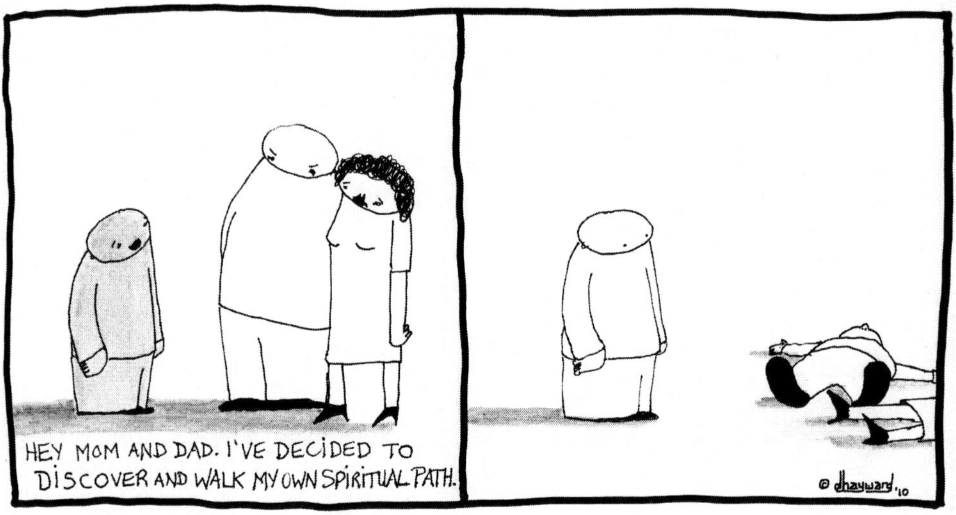
HEY MOM AND DAD. I'VE DECIDED TO DISCOVER AND WALK MY OWN SPIRITUAL PATH.
© dhayward '10

051

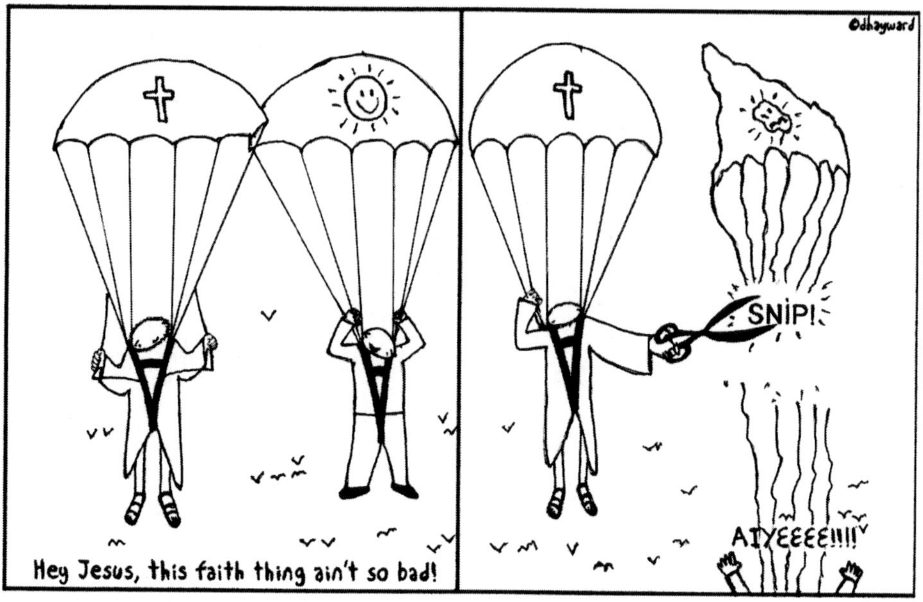
©dhayward
Hey Jesus, this faith thing ain't so bad!
SNIP!
AIYEEEE!!!!

There's always further to go when it comes to faith.

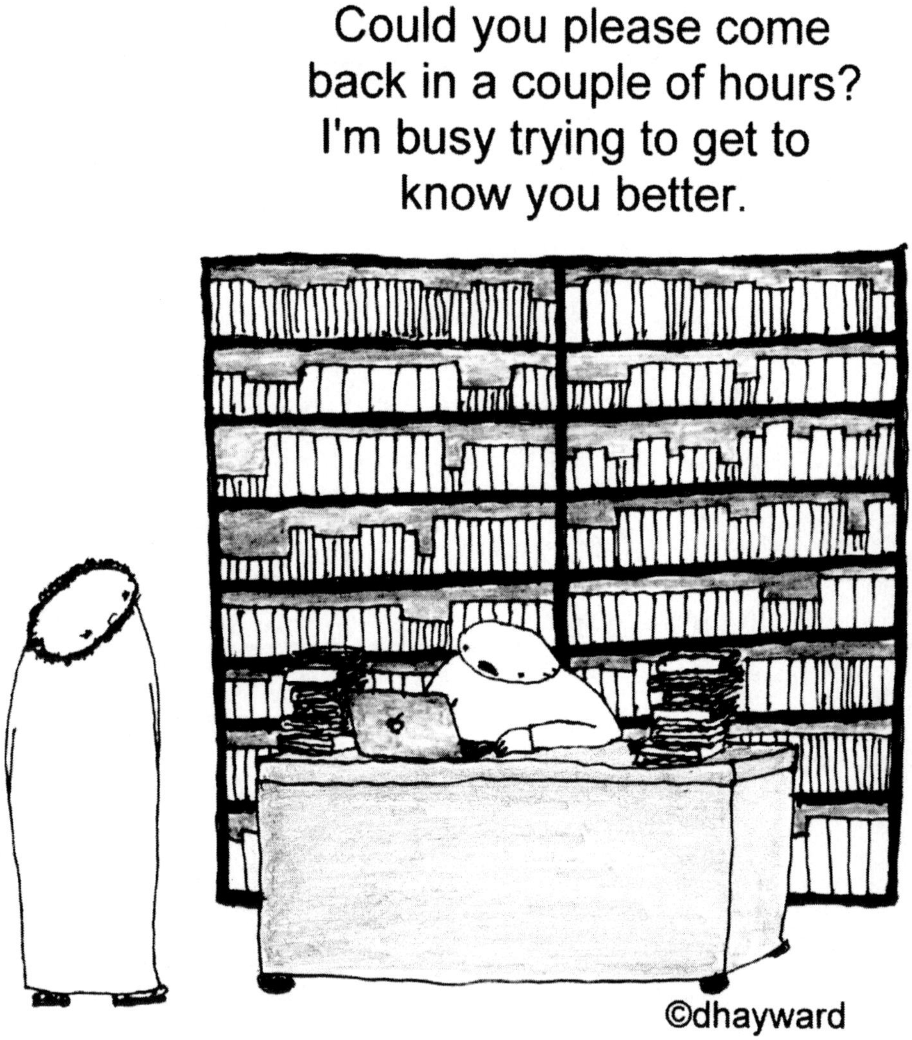
Could you please come back in a couple of hours? I'm busy trying to get to know you better.
©dhayward

Lisa has frequently pointed out to me that it is when I'm trying to be more spiritual that I actually become less so. Catch-22.

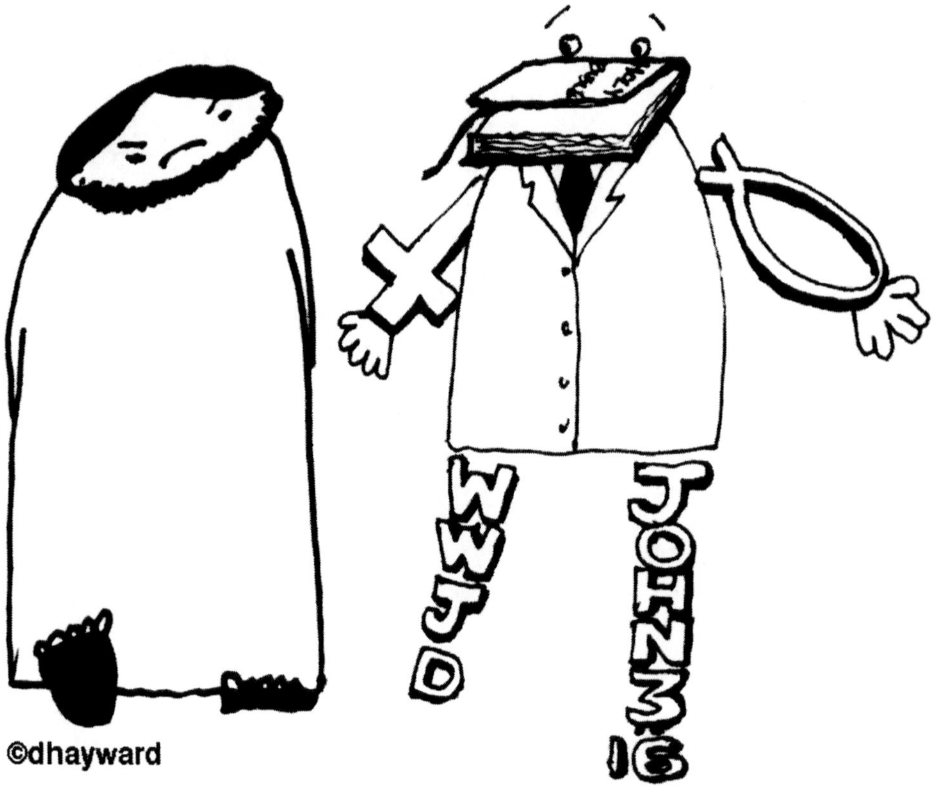
WWJD
JOHN3:16
©dhayward

The entire makeup of this guy's spirituality is a collection of popular clichés. Jesus is not happy.

054

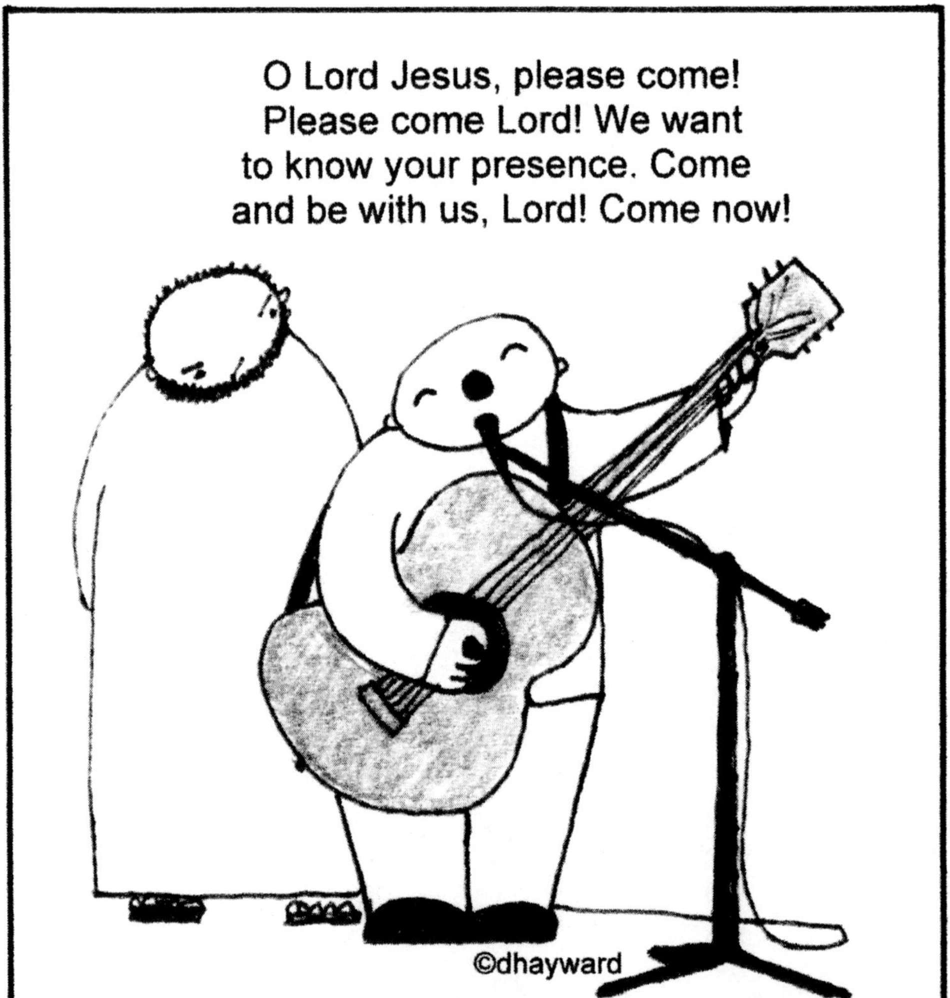
O Lord Jesus, please come! Please come Lord! We want to know your presence. Come and be with us, Lord! Come now!
©dhayward

This is one part of contemporary worship that I find really annoying: there is so much bad theology in it. Again, Jesus is not happy.

055

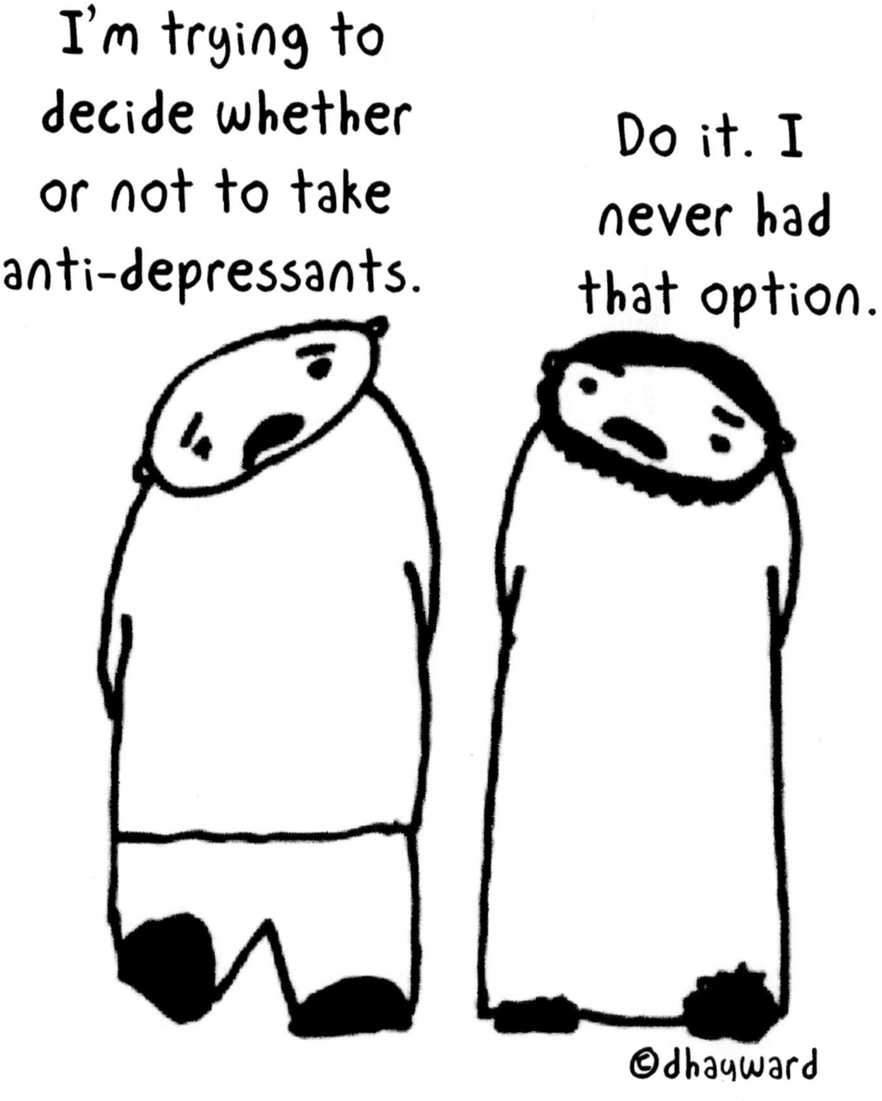
I'm trying to decide whether or not to take anti-depressants.
Do it. I never had that option.
©dhayward

I used to have a very negative opinion of drugs. But someone I love very much got very sick with anxiety, panic and depression. He got to the point where he was even bedridden. One day out of desperation he called the first psychiatrist in the yellow pages, made an appointment for that afternoon, and went and saw him. He had a session with the psychiatrist, completed a questionnaire that helped diagnose his problem, and was prescribed some drugs. The next day he woke up himself again, completely fine. It was like a miracle. My opinion about drugs changed.

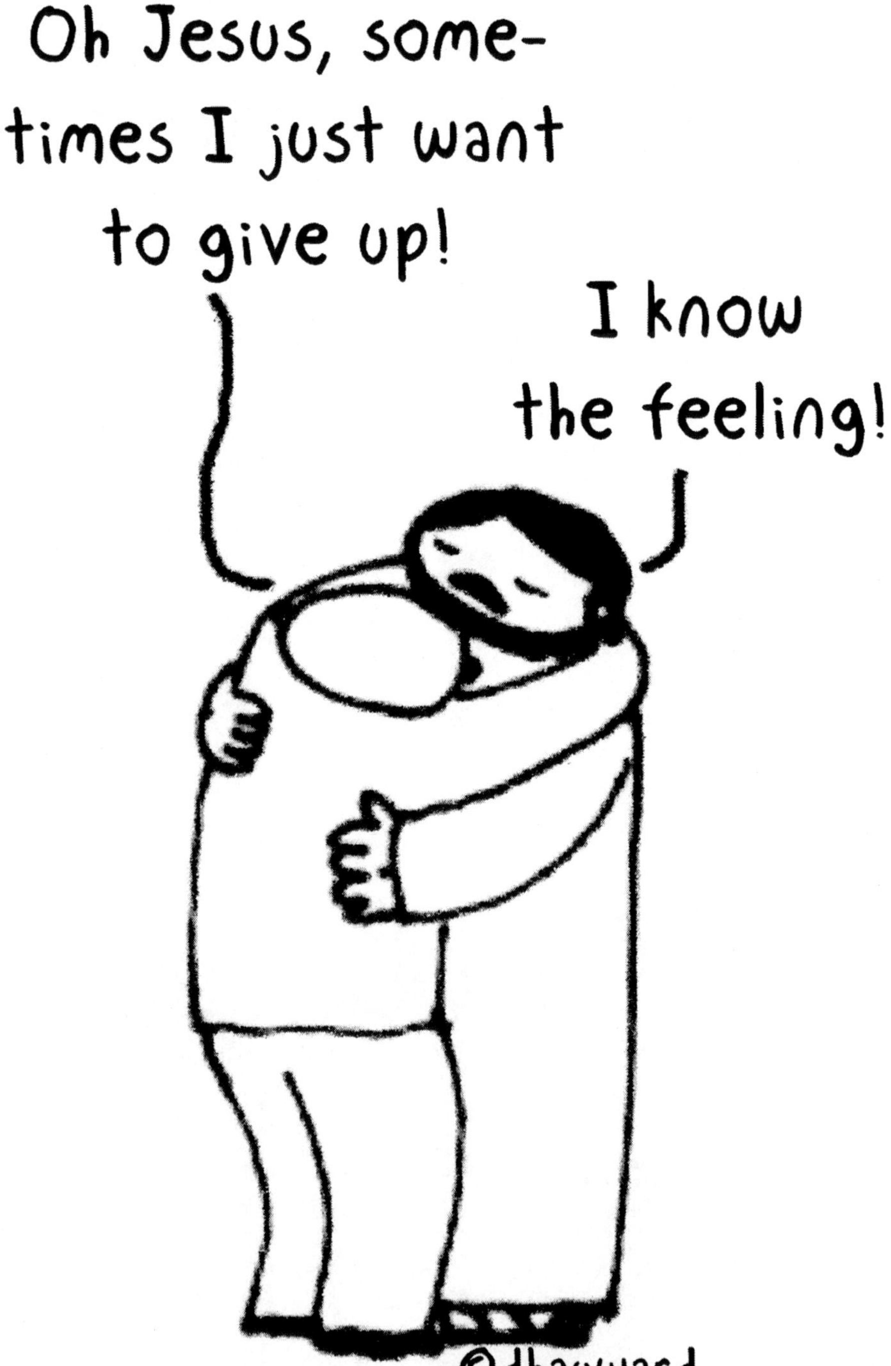
Oh Jesus, some-
times I just want
to give up!
I know
the feeling!
©dhayward

Do you mind?!
I'm trying to
read the Bible!
©dhayward

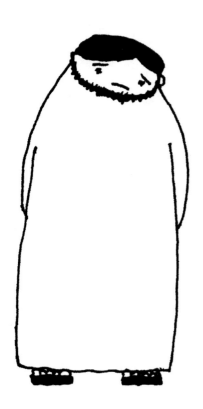

Sometimes your bible and Jesus have nothing in common.

"Personally, Don, I liked you a lot more before you became a Christian."

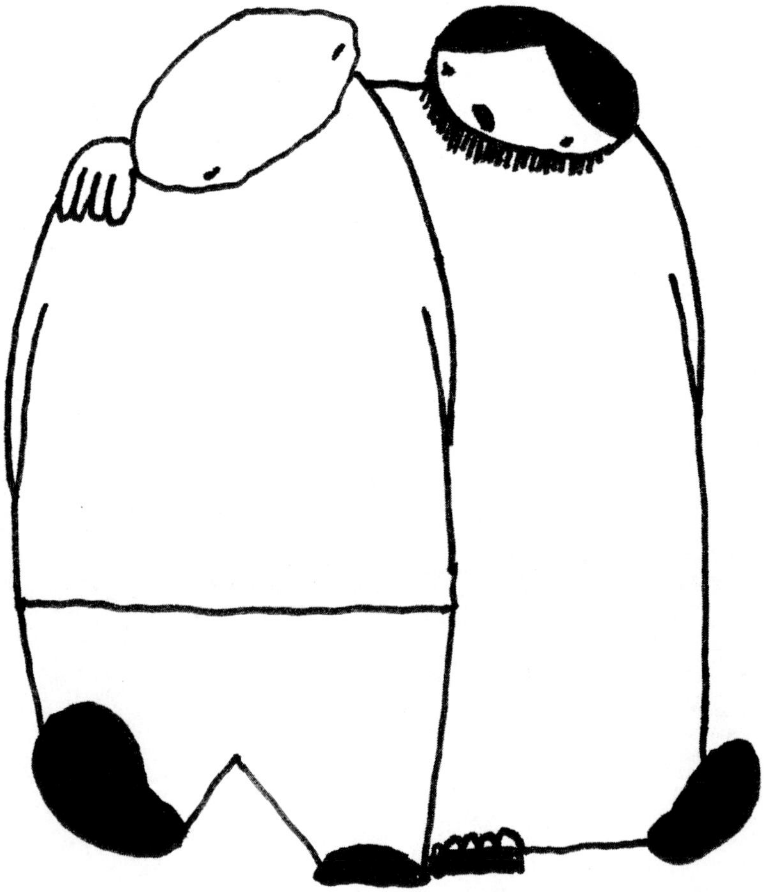
©dhayward10

The Real Left Behind

Didn't this cartoon just have to be drawn? The whole Left Behind phenomenon, in my opinion, has little to do with the Jesus of the gospels.

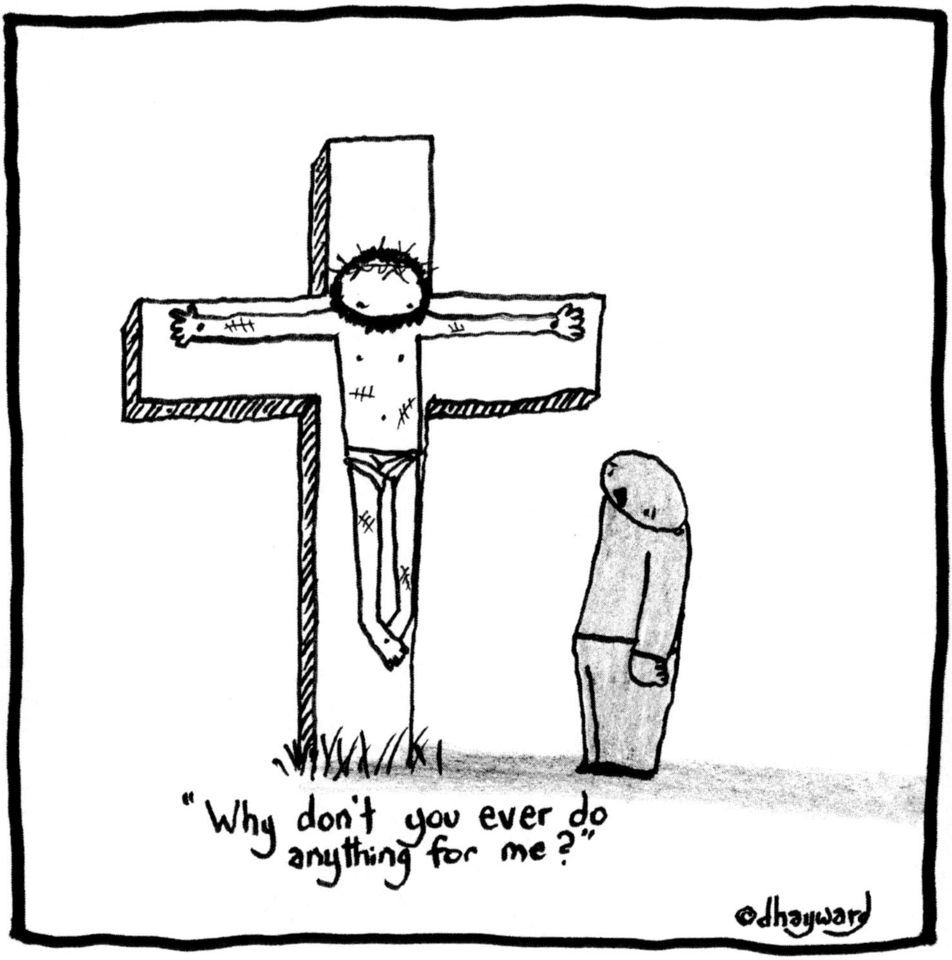
"Why don't you ever do anything for me?"
©dhayward

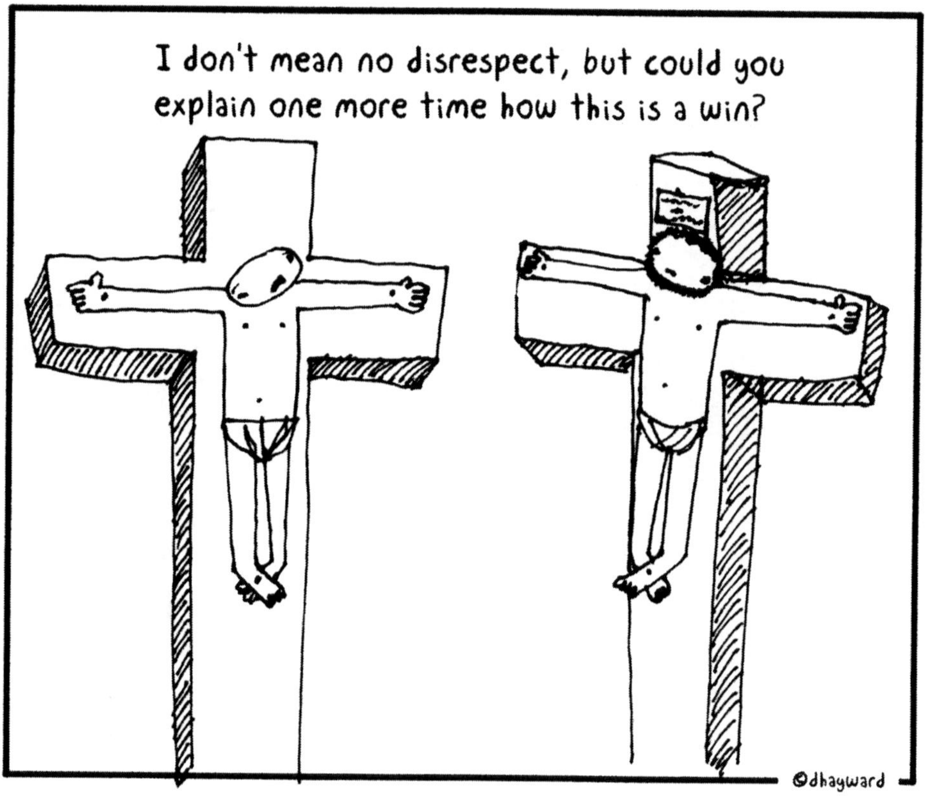
I don't mean no disrespect, but could you explain one more time how this is a win?
©dhayward

062

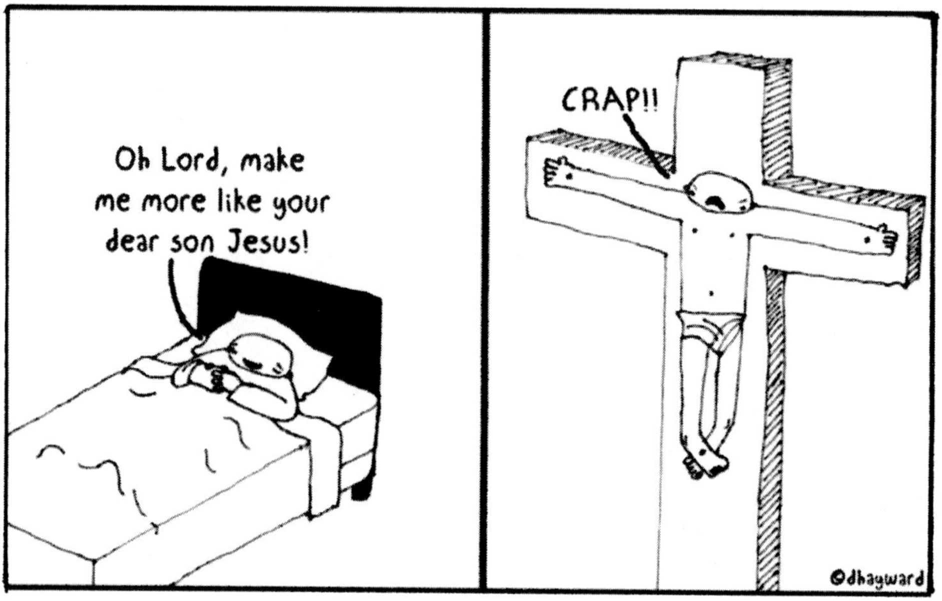
Oh Lord, make
me more like your
dear son Jesus!
CRAP!!
©dhayward

Be careful what you pray for.

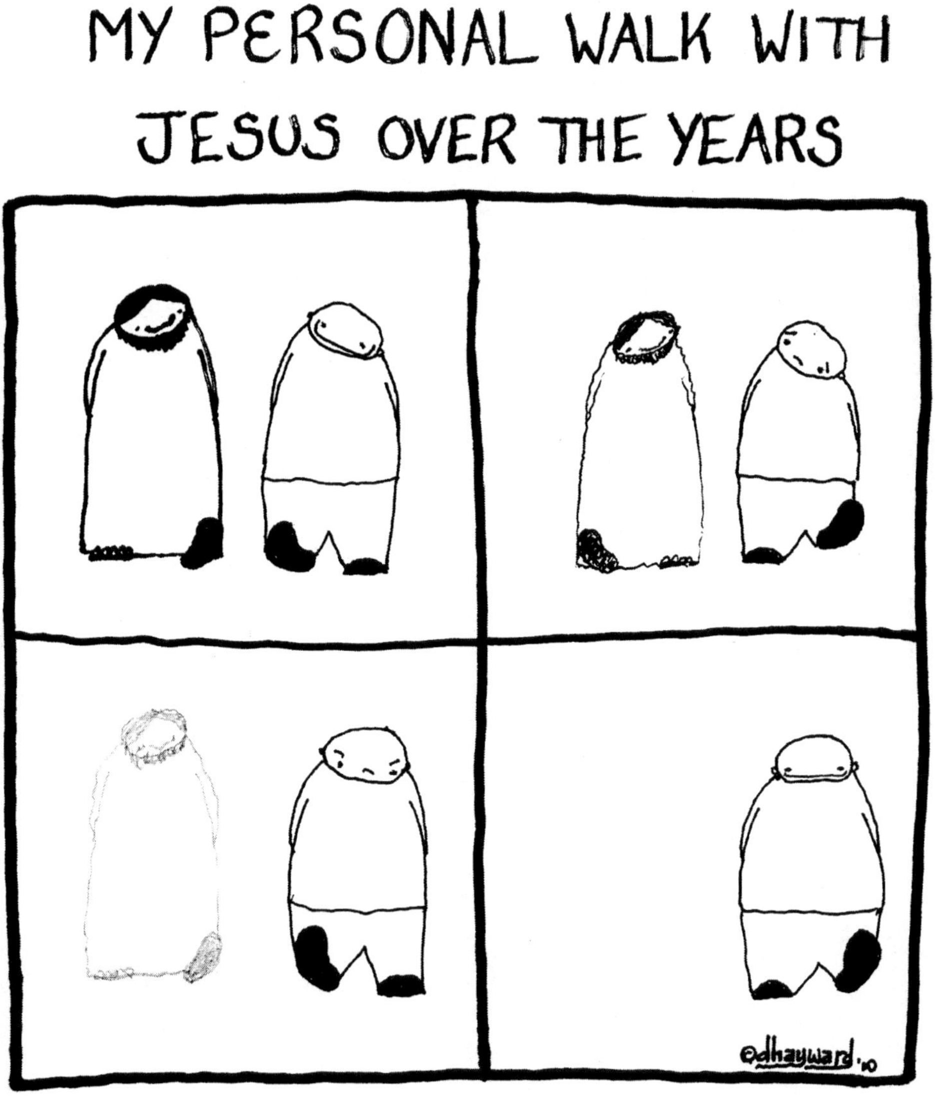
MY PERSONAL WALK WITH JESUS OVER THE YEARS
©dhayward.'10

Oh my, the controversy this stirred up. Some people thought I was saying that Jesus left my life, as in he's no longer in existence. But that's not necessarily what it means. The Jesus I walked with 30 years ago is not the Jesus I walk with today. Just think of the problems that last sentence creates.

God giving me a hand.
©dhayward

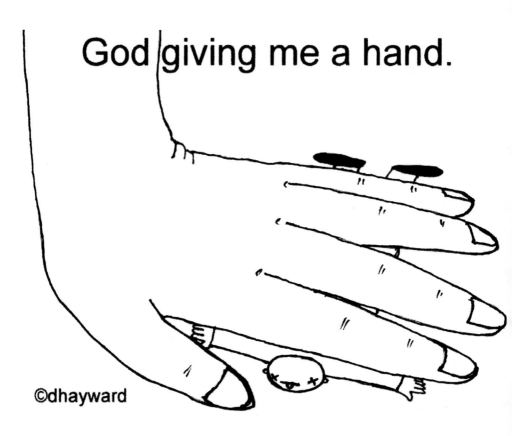

This is based upon 1 Peter 5:6, "Therefore humble yourselves under the mighty hand of God, that He may exalt you in due time, casting all your care upon Him, for He cares for you."

We used to be so close. Our relationship was intense! It was true love. But then he just started to drift away. Now he's gone, and I've lost hope that we will ever be together again.
Do you mind me asking his name?
God.
©dhayward10

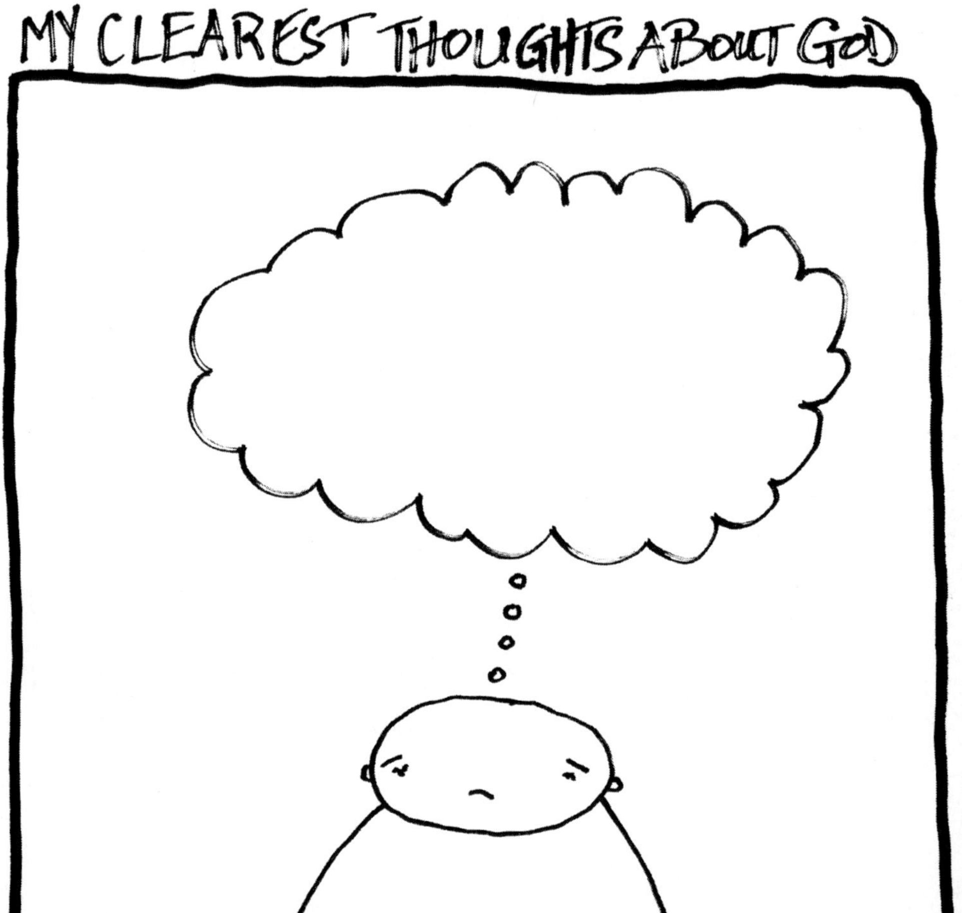
MY CLEAREST THOUGHTS ABOUT GOD
©dhayward

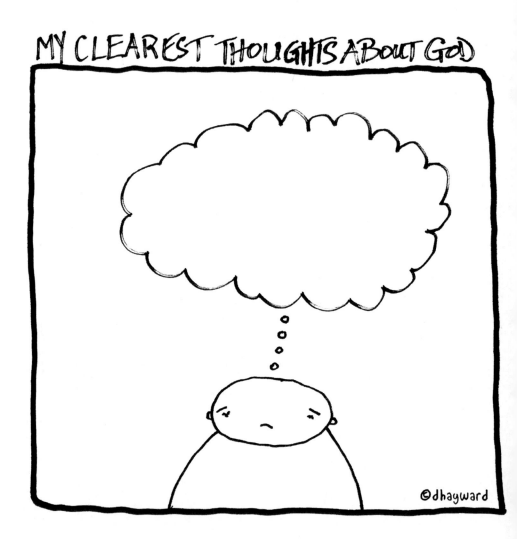

nakedpastor101
067

A snakehandler with sin in his life.

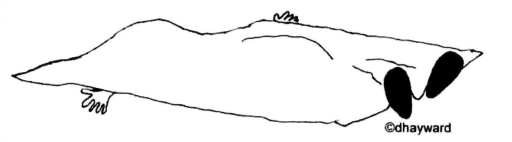

©dhayward

One day at breakfast while at a conference, I told this cartoon to a guy from the deep south and he laughed so hard he choked on his food.

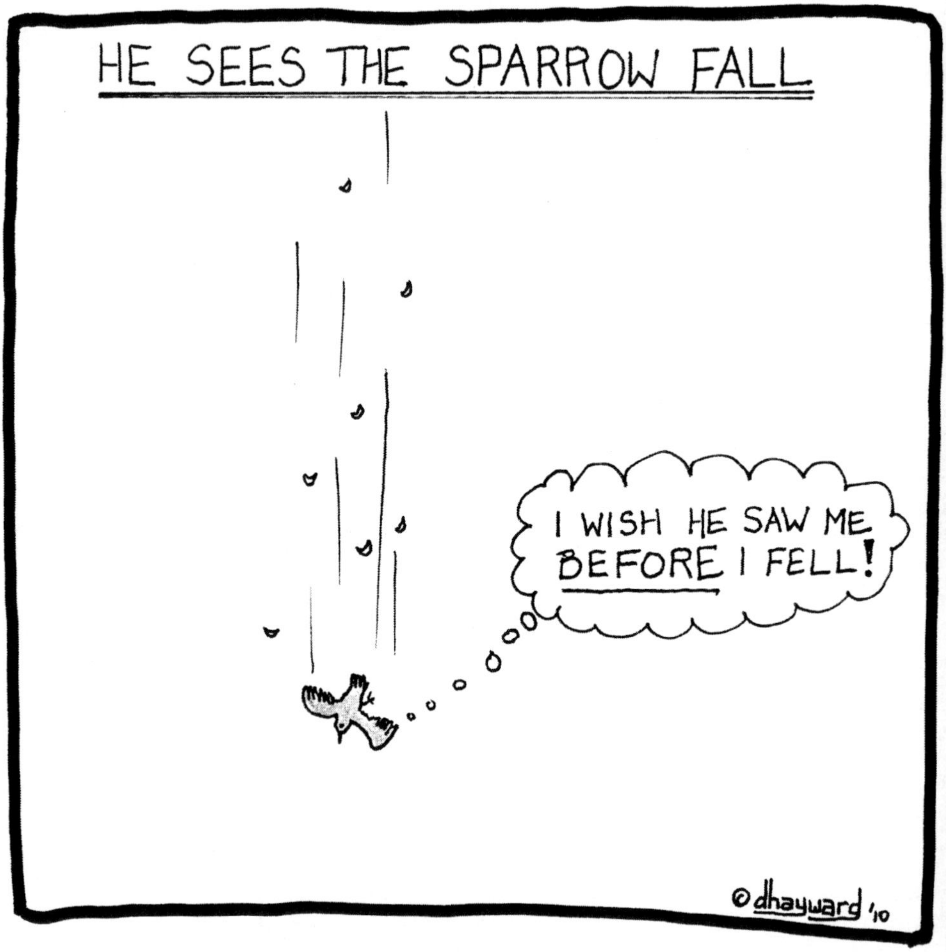
HE SEES THE SPARROW FALL
I WISH HE SAW ME BEFORE I FELL!
© dhayward '10

Jesus says that evidence that God intimately and personally cares for us is that he sees the little sparrow fall. I always wondered, since I was a little kid, how that sparrow must have felt.

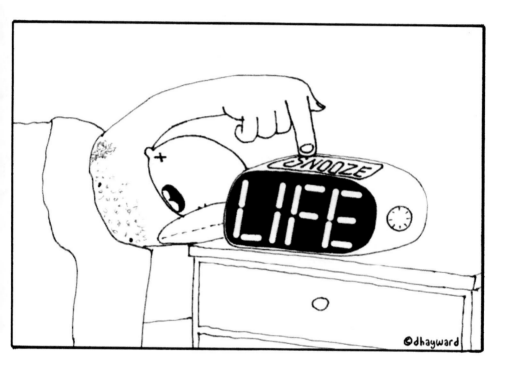

Many, many, many people are sleeping their way through life. Perpetual snooze.

Lazarus' favorite channel.

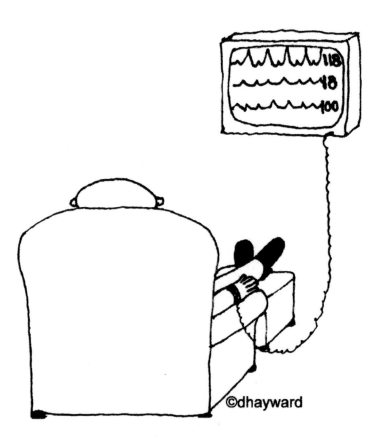

Just think of how much more vibrant life must have been for Lazarus! Every taste, every smell, every touch, even breath itself. It must have been exhilarating.

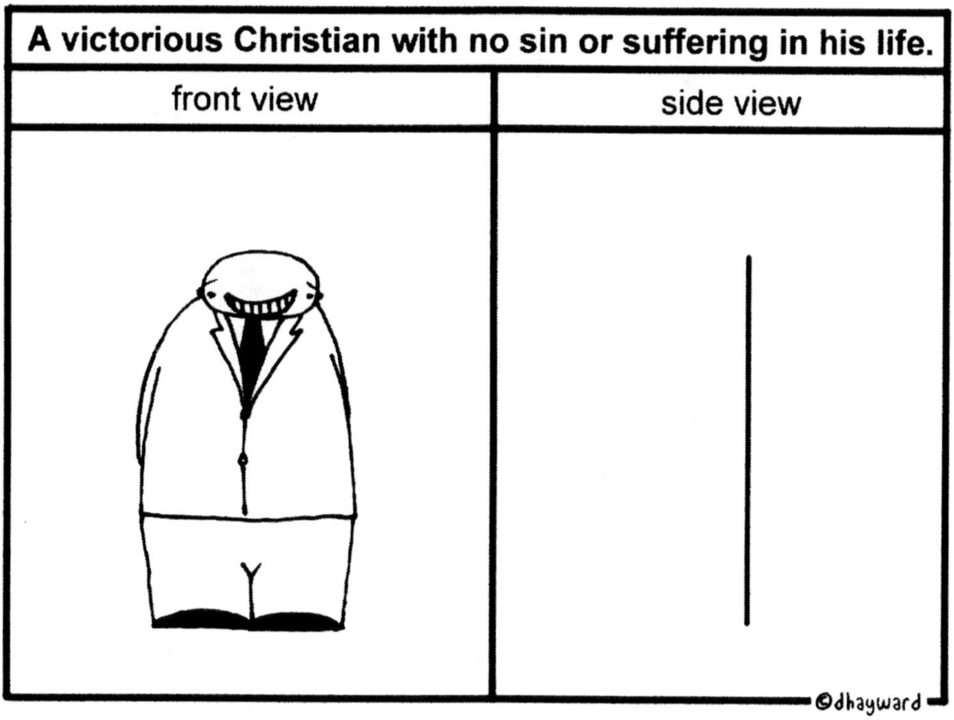
A victorious Christian with no sin or suffering in his life.
front view
side view
©dhayward

072

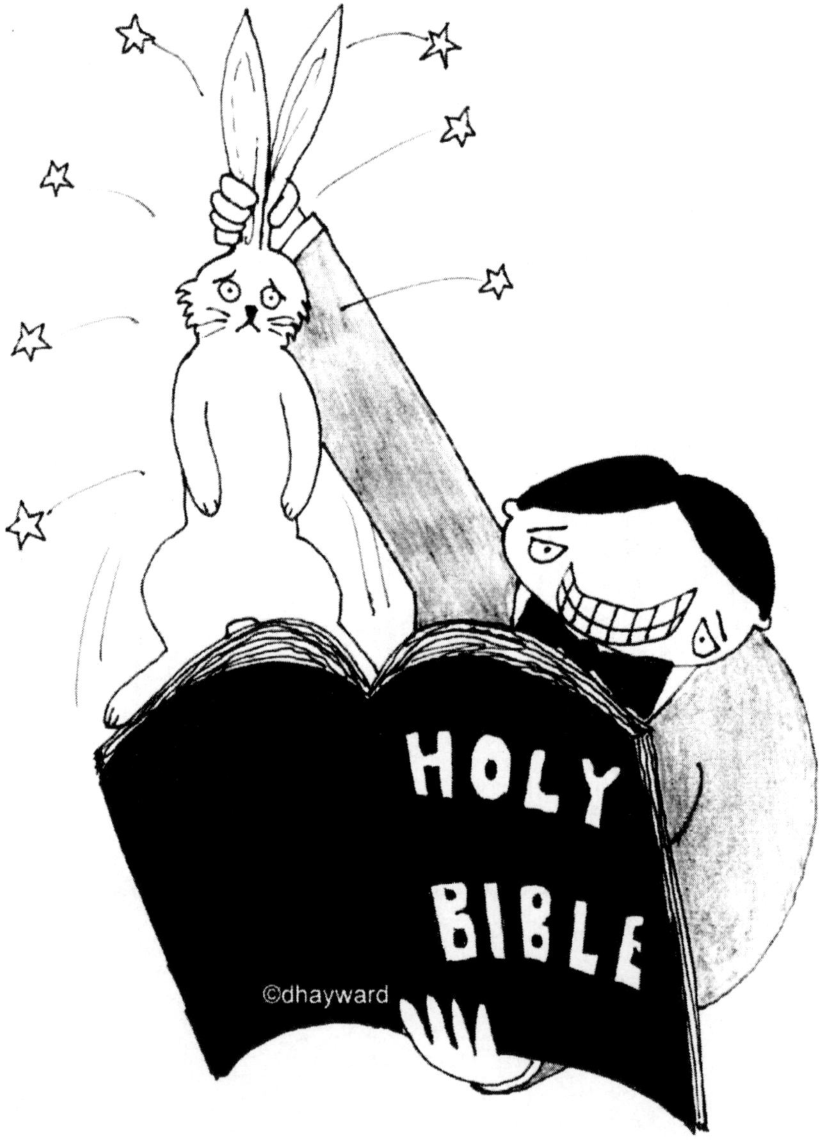
HOLY
BIBLE
©dhayward

Many treat the bible like it's magic. It ain't.

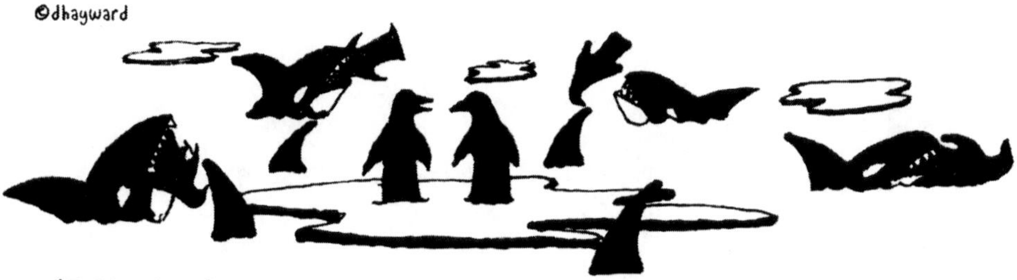
©dhayward

"I think it's time to claim by faith that this isn't happening!"

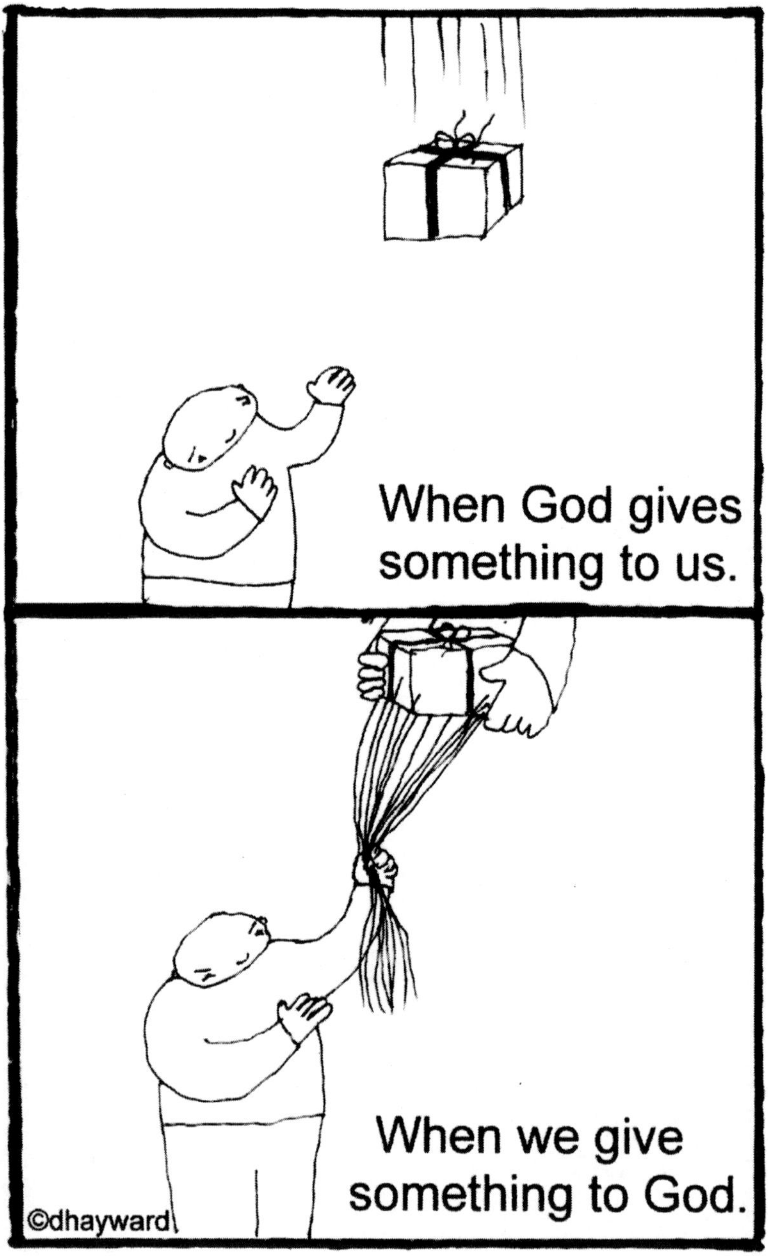
When God gives something to us.
When we give something to God.
©dhayward

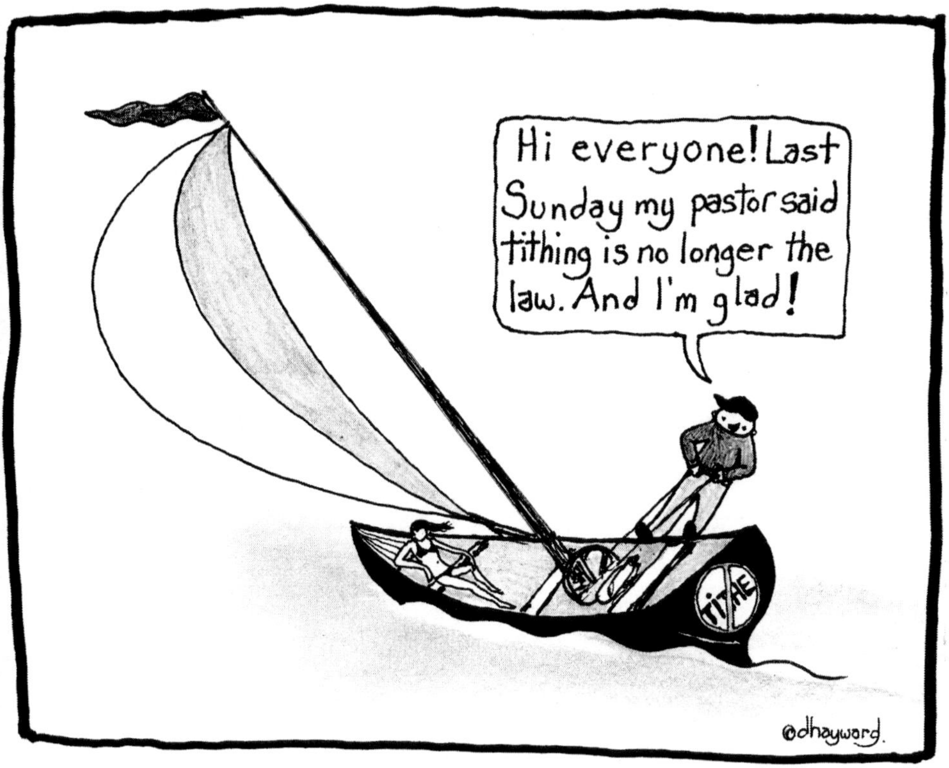
Hi everyone! Last Sunday my pastor said tithing is no longer the law. And I'm glad!
TITHE
©dhayward.

This is based on something a friend wrote in my farewell book the last church gave to me when I resigned. He wrote, "Thanks for teaching us that tithing is no longer the law. I love my sailboat!"

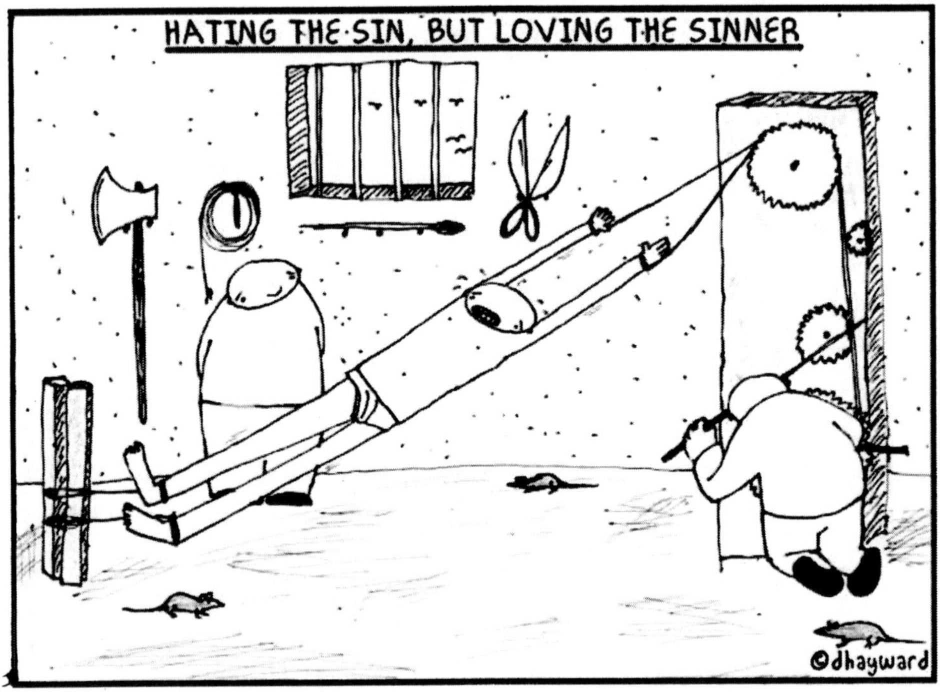
HATING THE SIN, BUT LOVING THE SINNER
©dhayward

It takes a very fine spiritual surgeon to separate the sin from the sinner. During the Inquisition they were called Inquisitors… torturers… experts in this art. Yet separating the weeds from the wheat is something so many love to try their hand at.

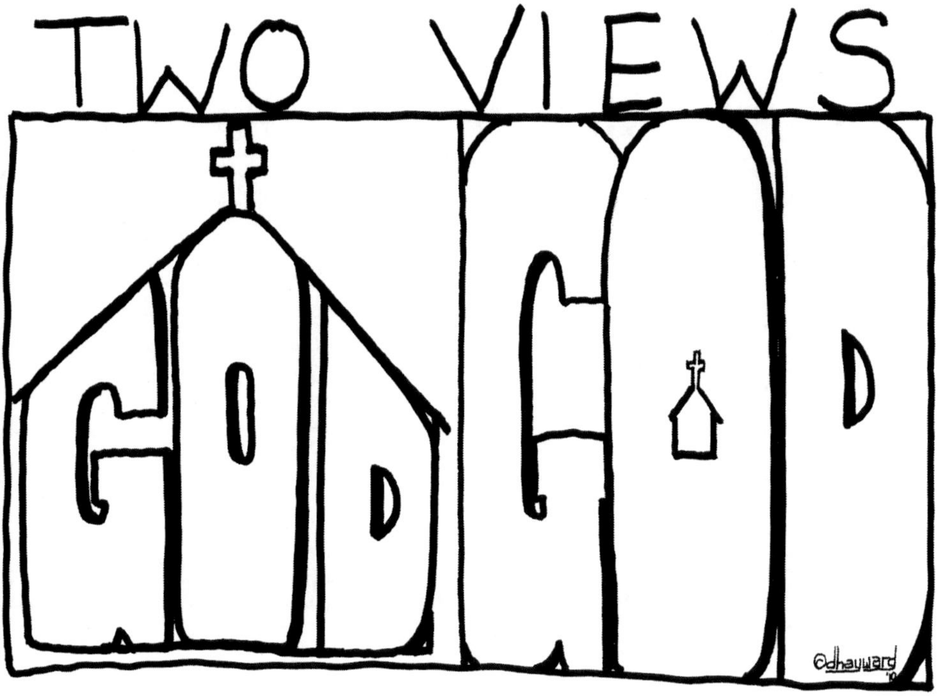
TWO VIEWS
GOD
GOD
©dhayward '10

A good friend of mine suggested that I do another box around this cartoon and title that God too. I mean, we could go on and on.

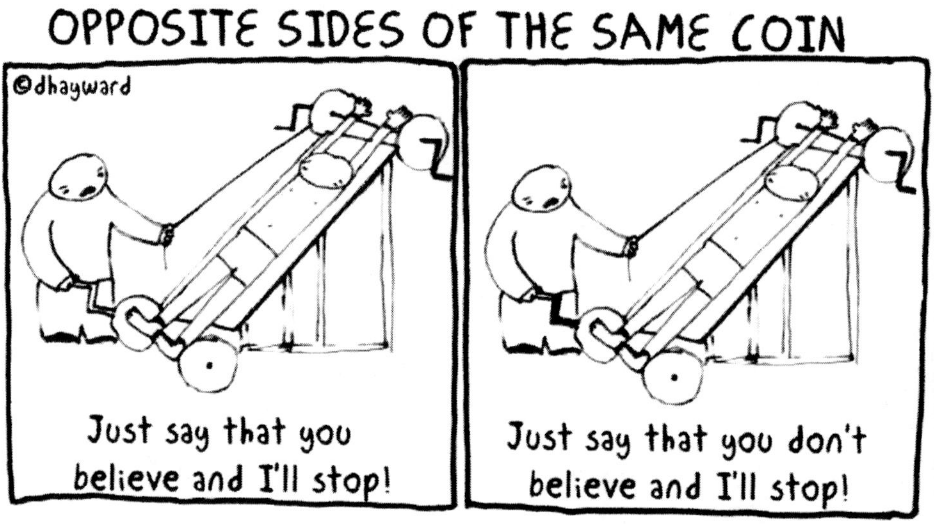
OPPOSITE SIDES OF THE SAME COIN
©dhayward
Just say that you believe and I'll stop!
Just say that you don't believe and I'll stop!

It was quite an experience for me to read Sam Harris' book, The End of Faith, in which he actually endorses torture. I realized then that fundamentalism knows no bounds and is not just confined to religion. Chris Hedges, in his book "I Don't Believe in Atheists" would agree. The problem isn't the religion, but the fundamentalist mindset.

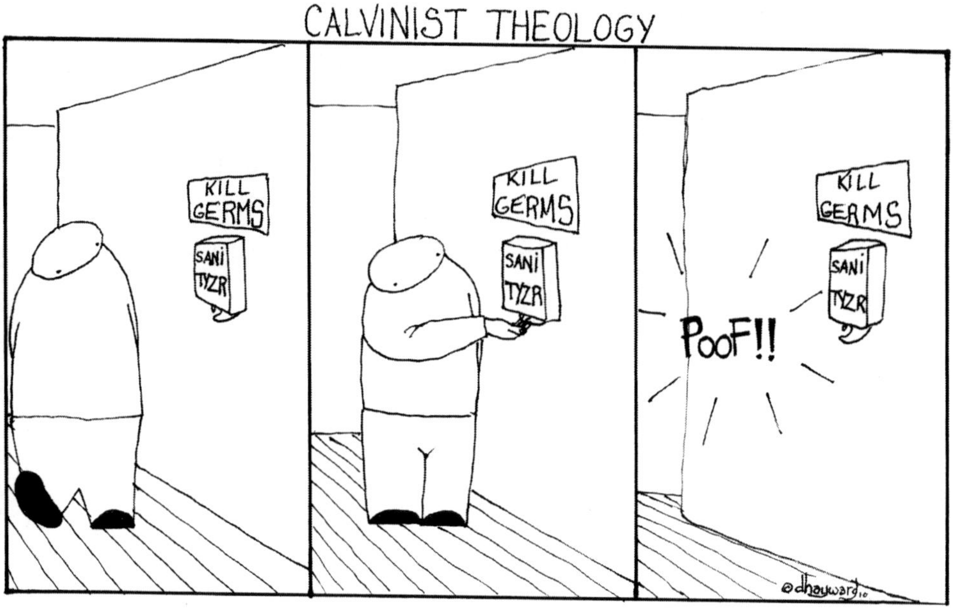
CALVINIST THEOLOGY
KILL GERMS
SANI TYZR
KILL GERMS
SANI TYZR
KILL GERMS
SANI TYZR
PooF!!
©dhayward.10

080

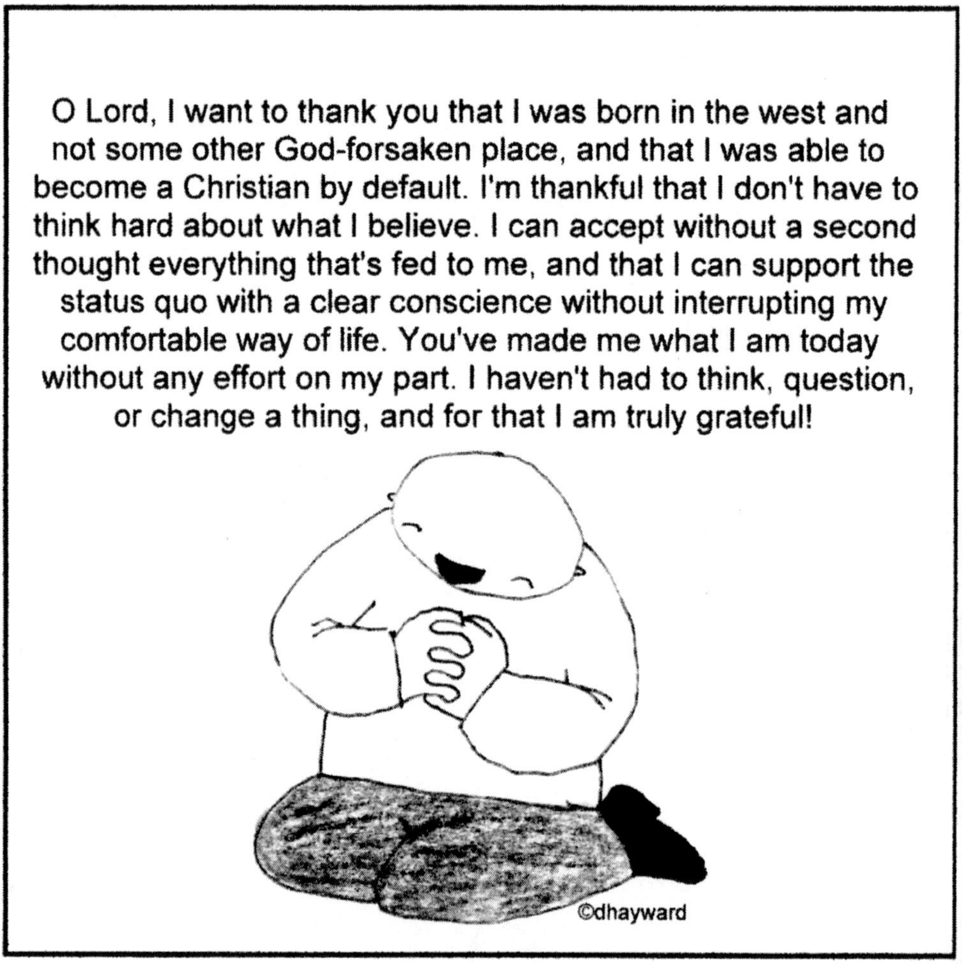
O Lord, I want to thank you that I was born in the west and not some other God-forsaken place, and that I was able to become a Christian by default. I'm thankful that I don't have to think hard about what I believe. I can accept without a second thought everything that's fed to me, and that I can support the status quo with a clear conscience without interrupting my comfortable way of life. You've made me what I am today without any effort on my part. I haven't had to think, question, or change a thing, and for that I am truly grateful!
©dhayward

This one got stumbled-upon and went everywhere on the web. Fun to watch.

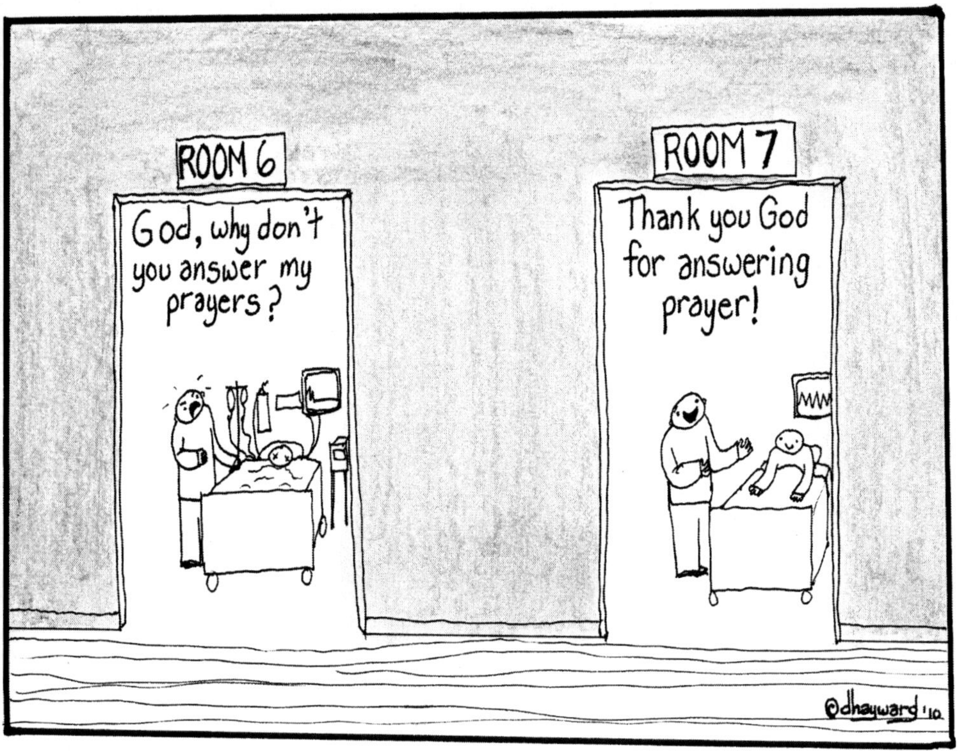
ROOM 6
God, why don't you answer my prayers?
ROOM 7
Thank you God for answering prayer!
©dhayward '10

This cartoon was inspired by something that happened on Facebook. On one person's update, they were rejoicing that God always answers prayers and healed her son. Another person's update was grief-stricken because she had just lost hers.

THE OCEAN OF GOD'S LOVE
you are here
©dhayward.10

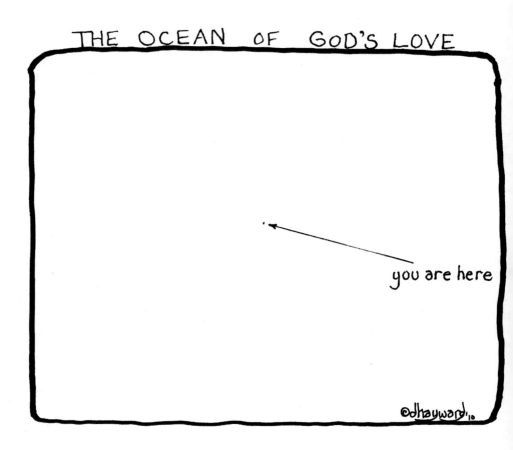

LITTLE PEOPLE AND BIG PICTURES
ZOOM IN
ZOOM OUT
God, where are you?
©dhayward

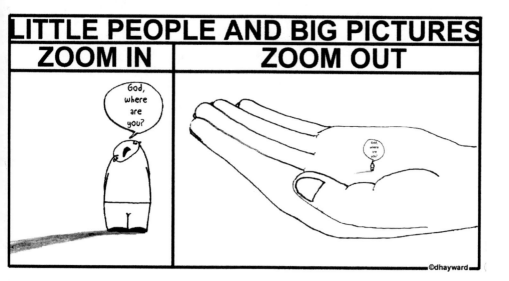

Sometimes it's all a matter of perspective.

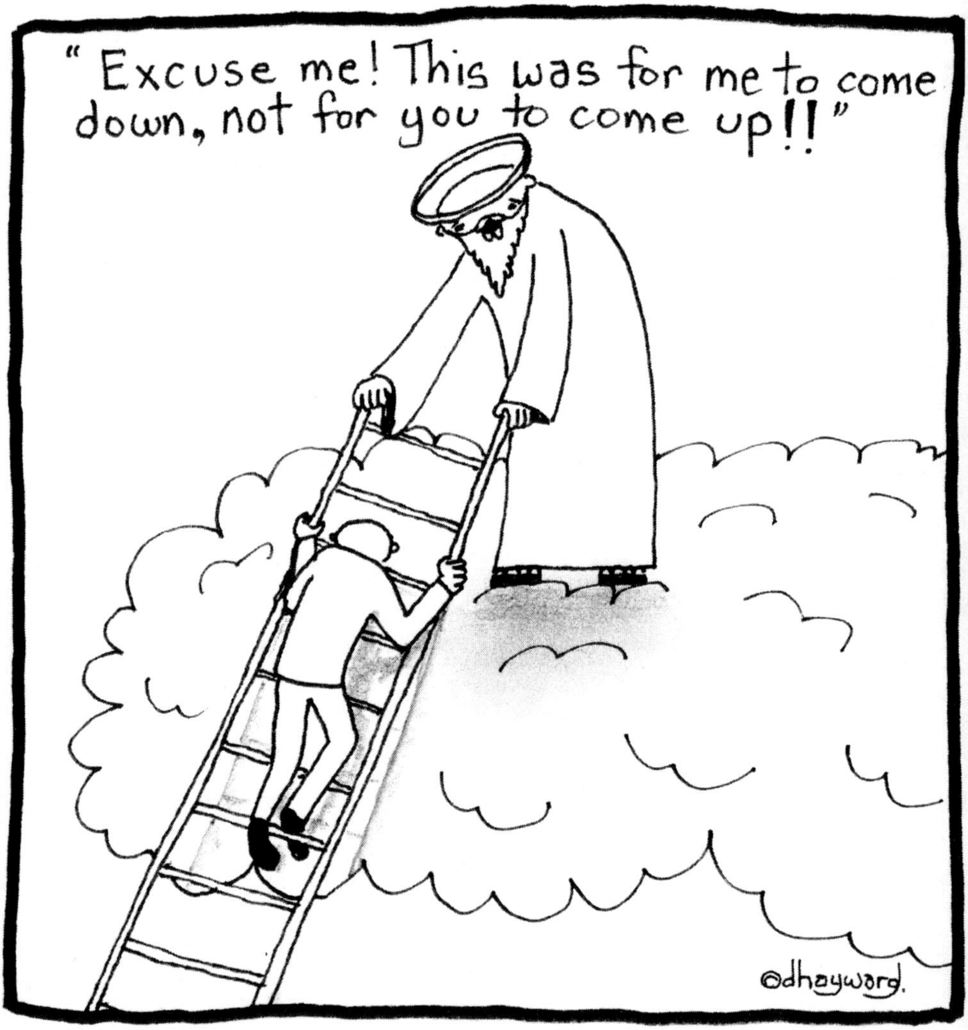
"Excuse me! This was for me to come down, not for you to come up!!"
©dhayward.

I remember when I was a kid at Vacation Bible School, the teacher taught us about Jacob's ladder. She read the story. I asked the question, "But isn't the ladder for the angels to come down and go up? It's not for Jacob." I got in trouble for that.

A FLY ON THE WALL

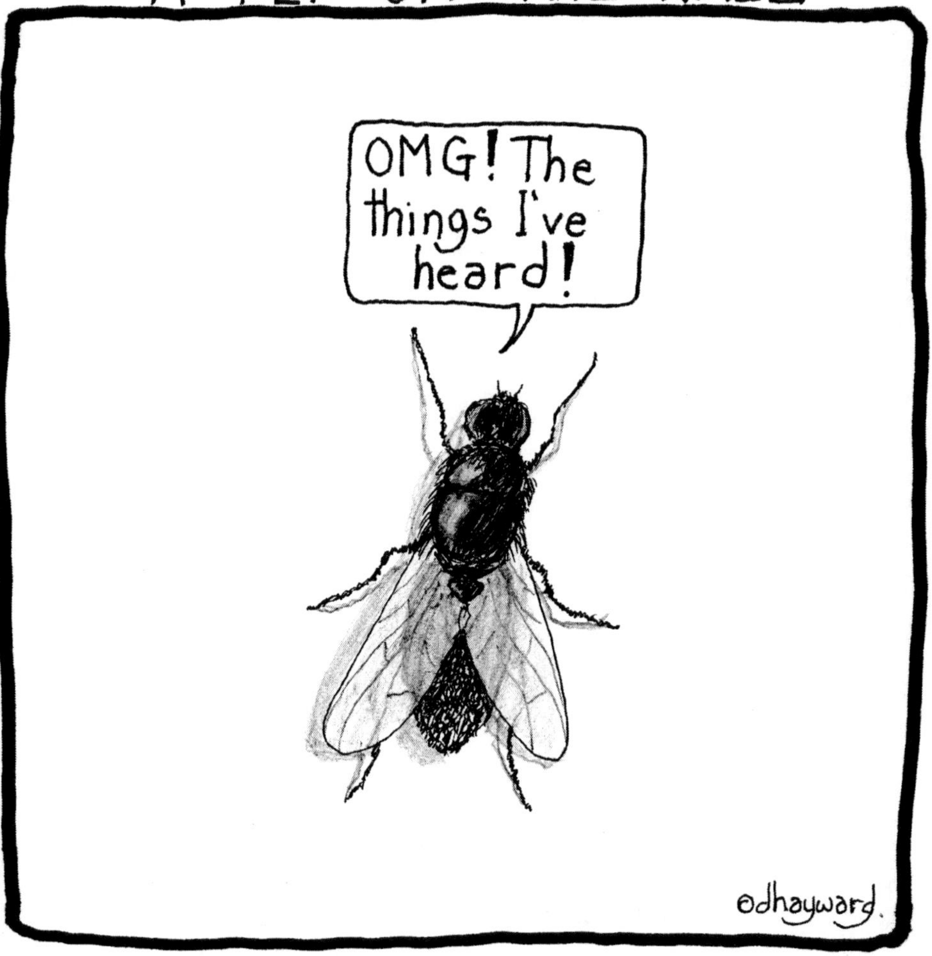
OMG! The things I've heard!
©dhayward.

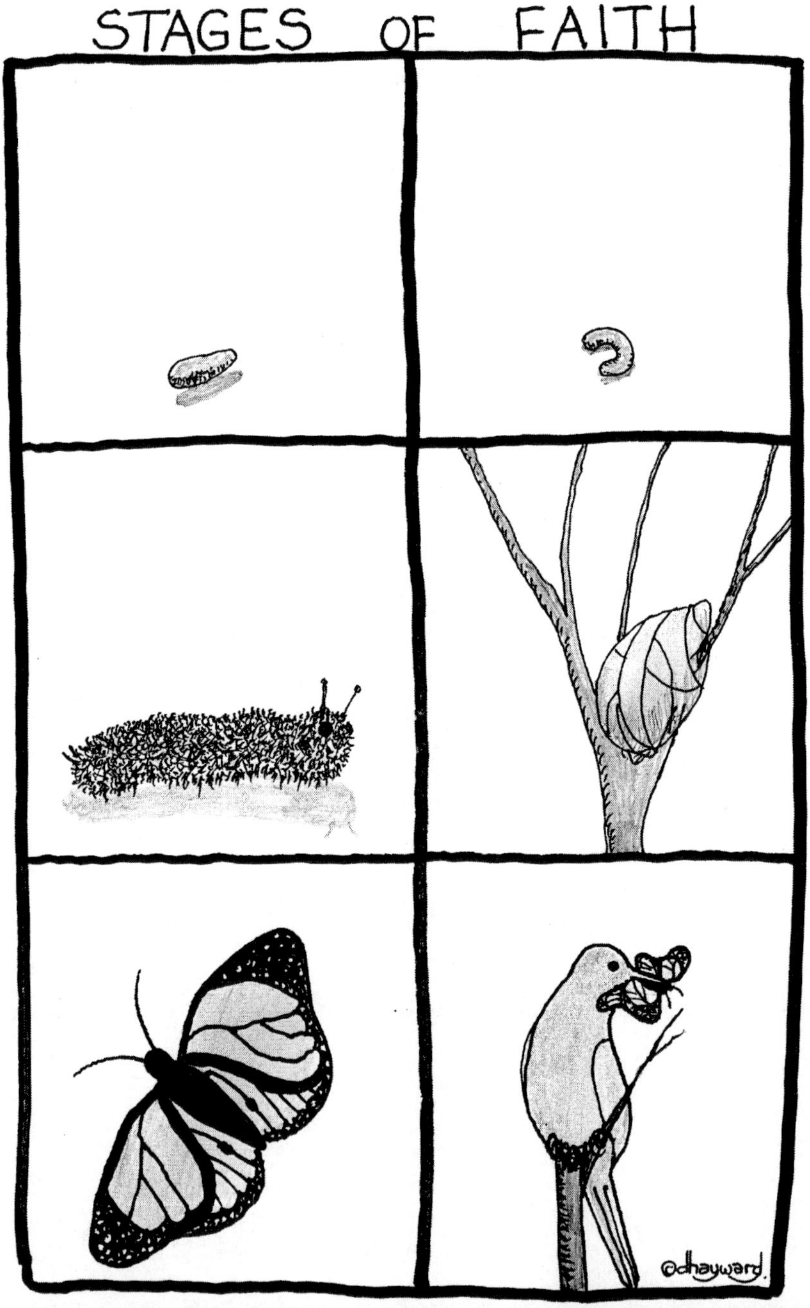
STAGES OF FAITH
©dhayward

Egg. Larva. Caterpillar. Cocoon. Butterfly. Sacrifice.

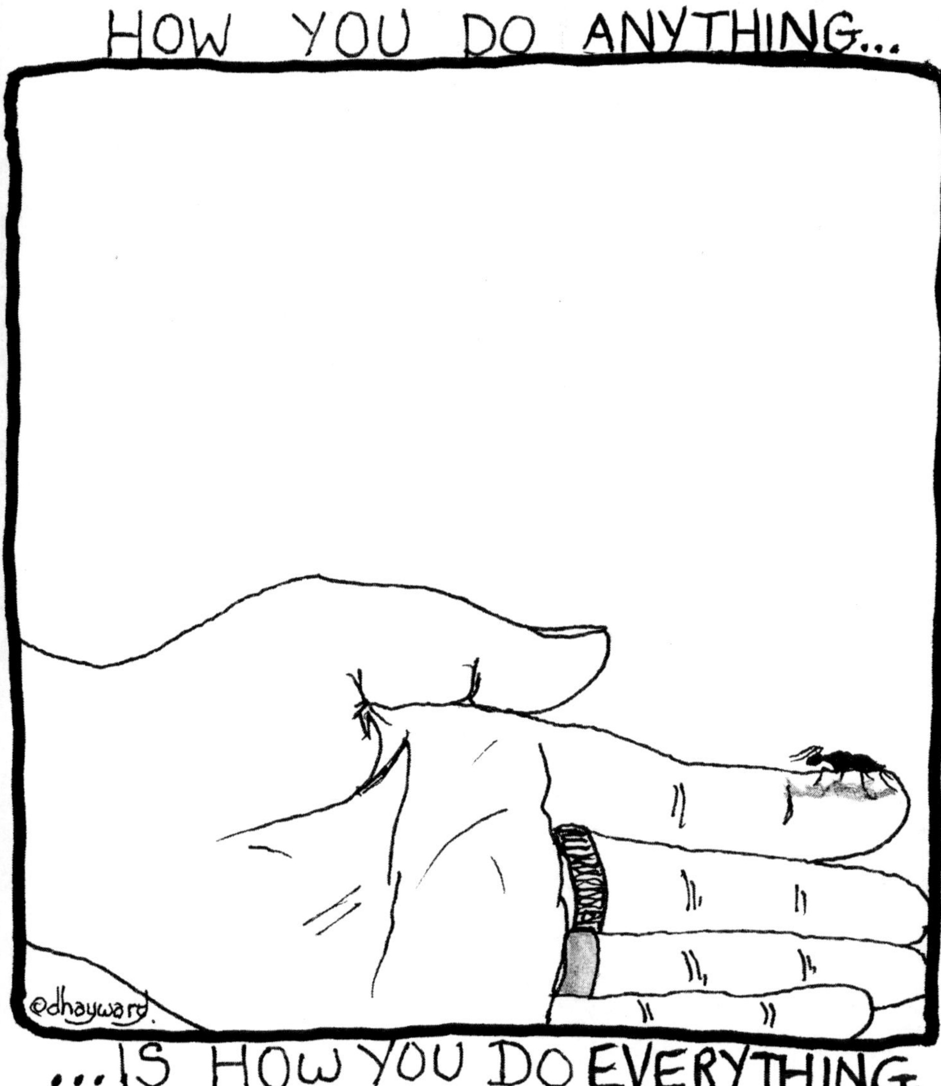
HOW YOU DO ANYTHING...
©dhayward.
...IS HOW YOU DO EVERYTHING.

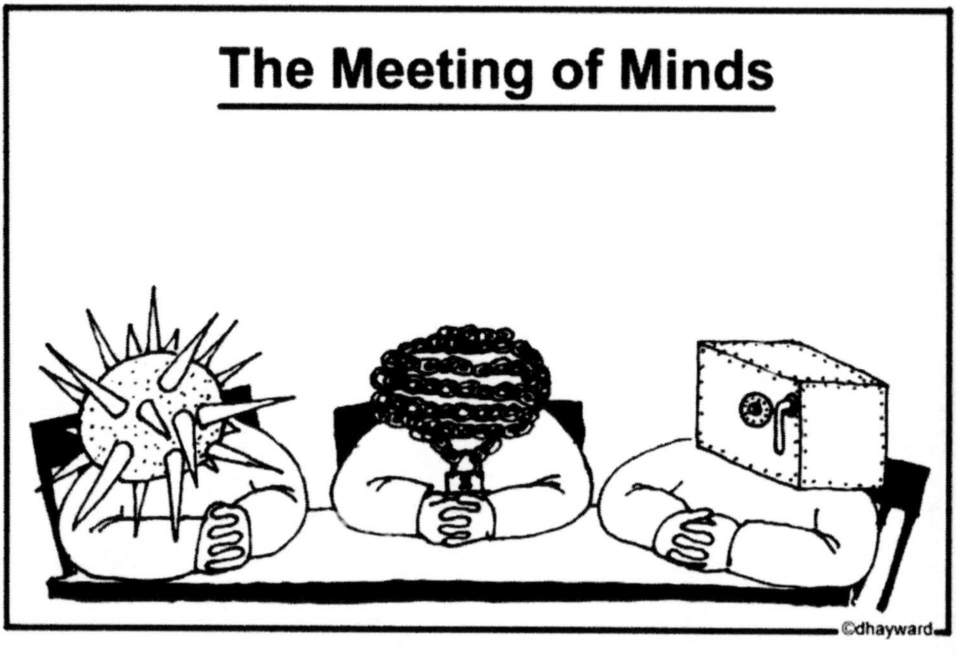
The Meeting of Minds
©dhayward

Sometimes dialog seems impossible, mainly because the participants refuse to participate.

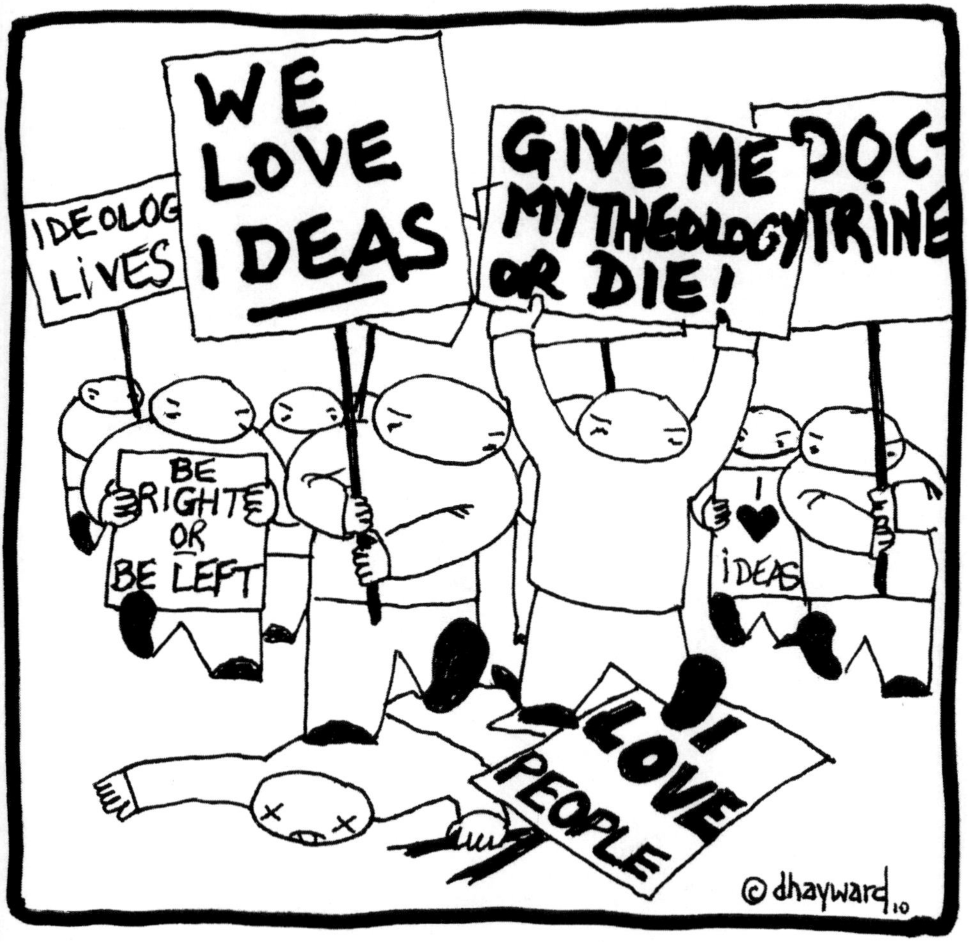
IDEOLOG
LIVES
WE
LOVE
IDEAS
GIVE ME
MY THEOLOGY
OR DIE!
DOC-
TRINE
BE
RIGHT
OR
BE LEFT
I ♥ IDEAS
I
LOVE
PEOPLE
© dhayward 10

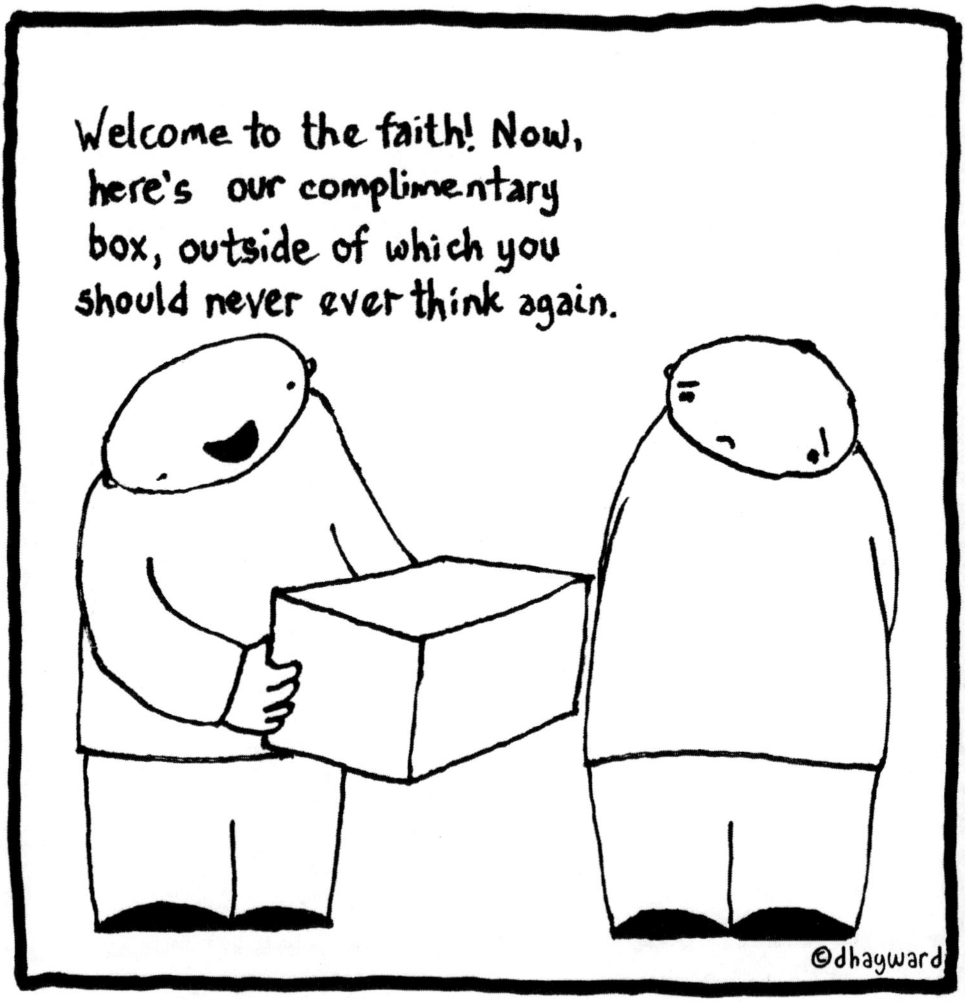
Welcome to the faith! Now, here's our complimentary box, outside of which you should never ever think again.
©dhayward

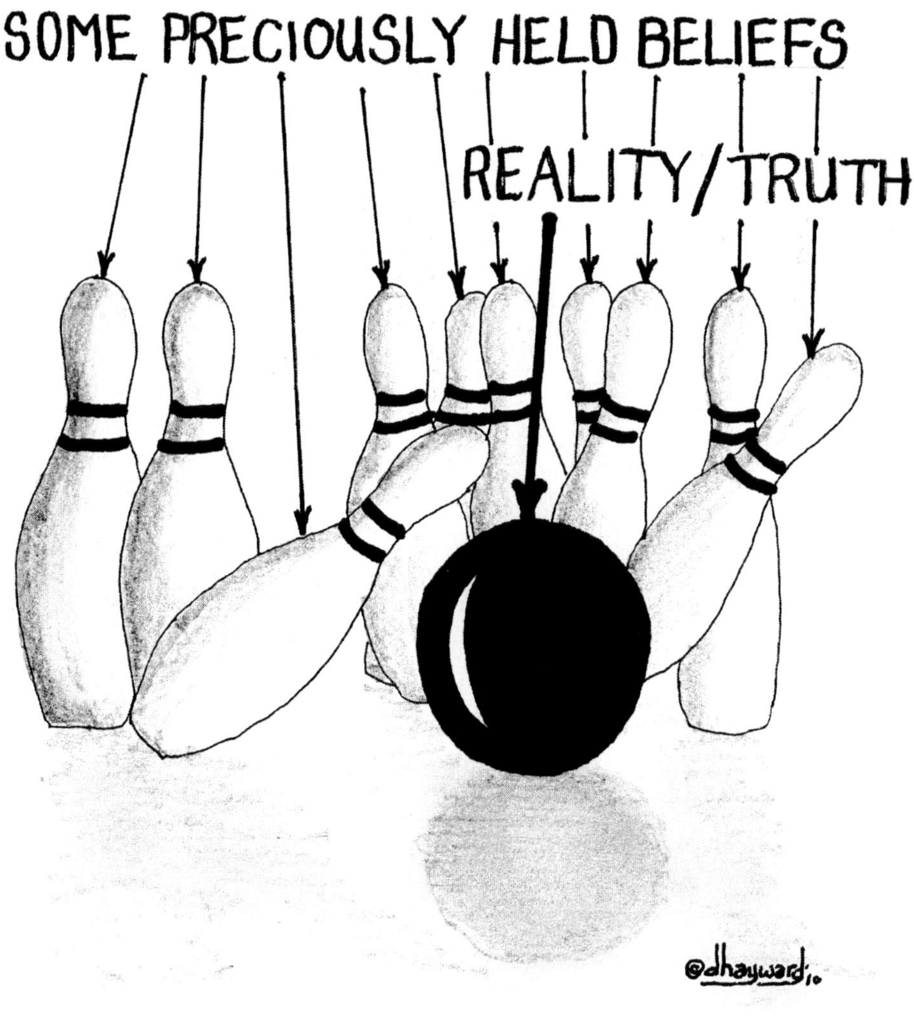
SOME PRECIOUSLY HELD BELIEFS
REALITY/TRUTH
©dhayward10

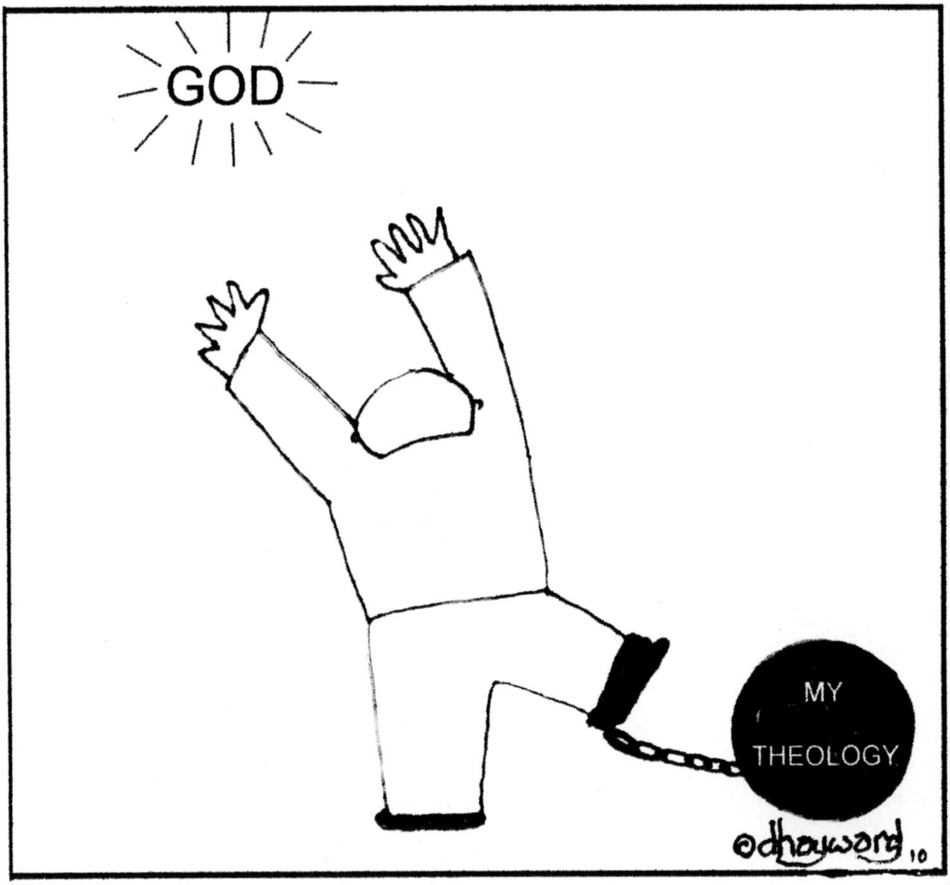
GOD
MY THEOLOGY
©dhayward 10

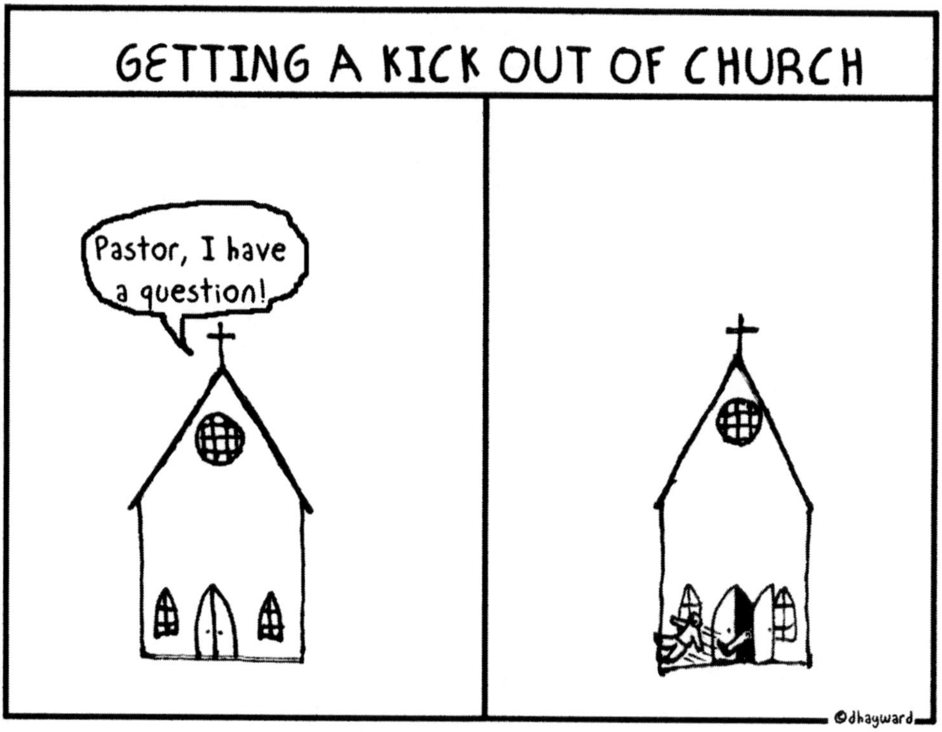
GETTING A KICK OUT OF CHURCH
Pastor, I have a question!
©dhayward

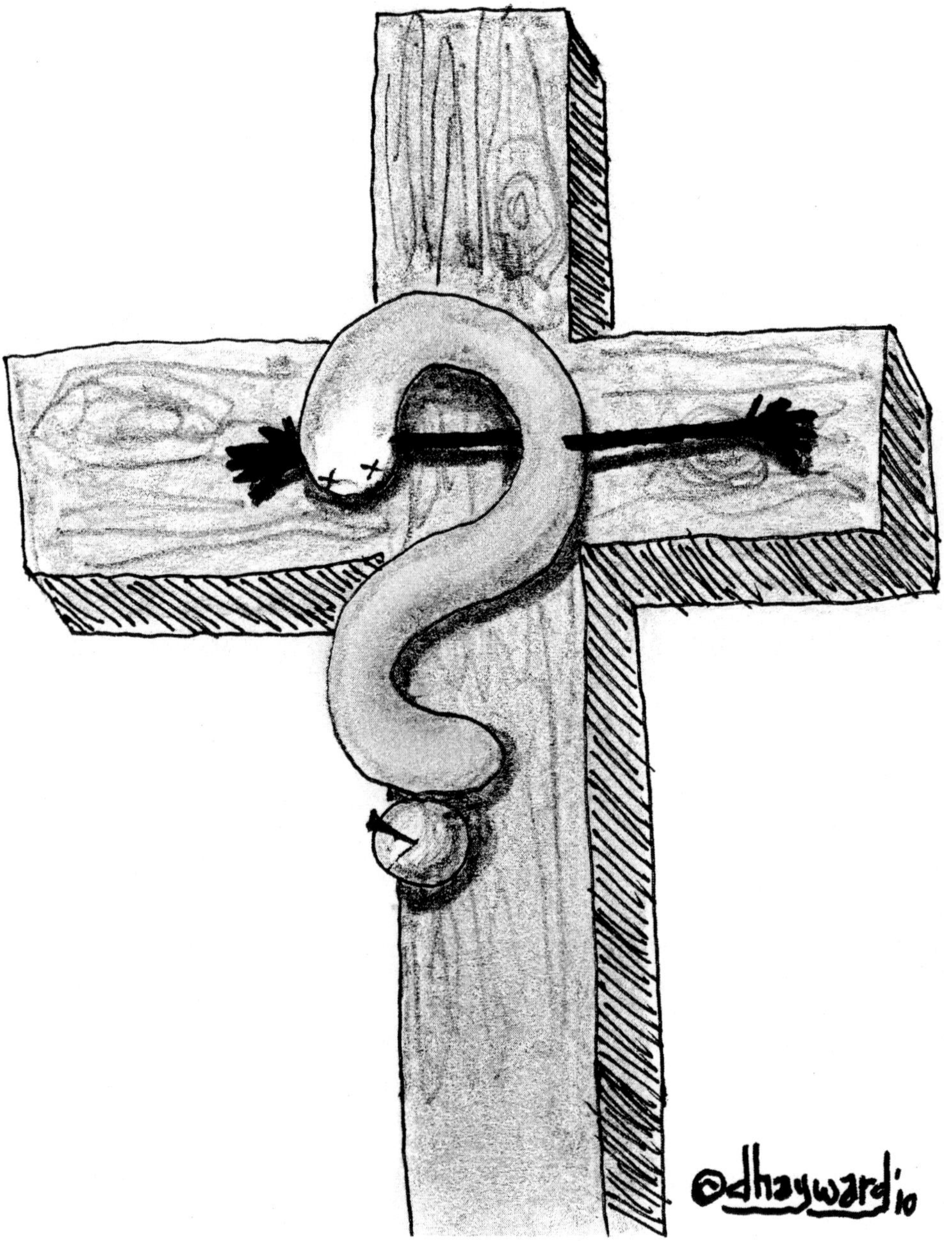
@dhayward'10

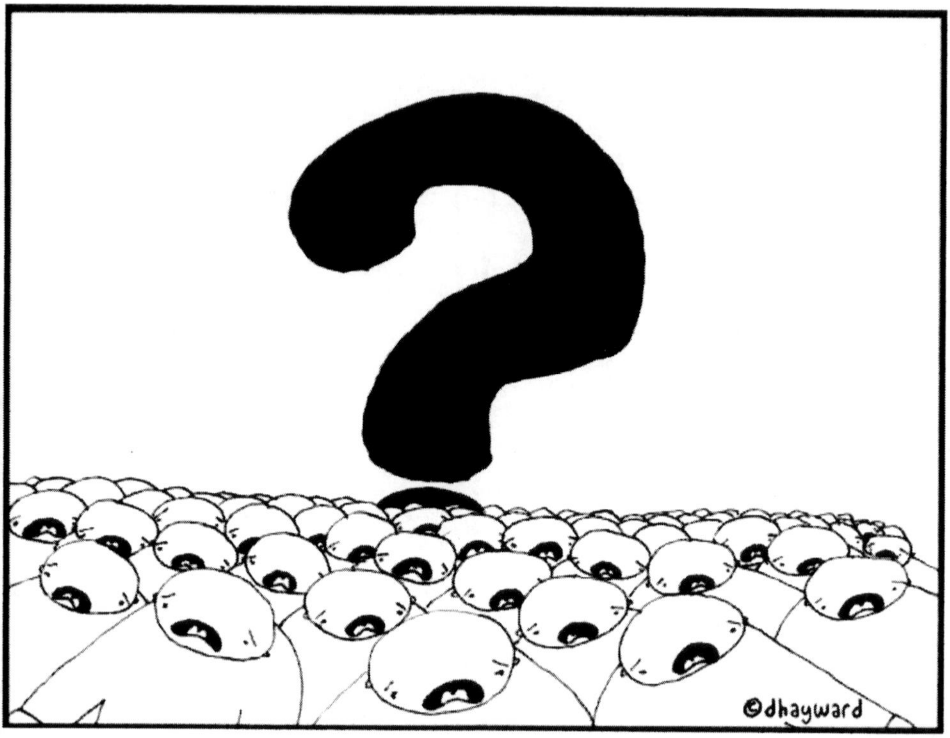
©dhayward

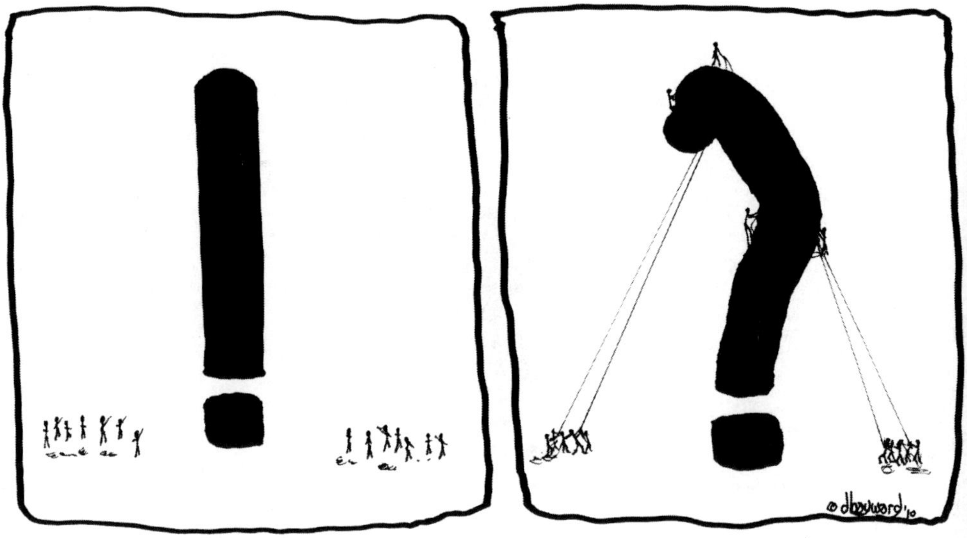
© dhayward '10

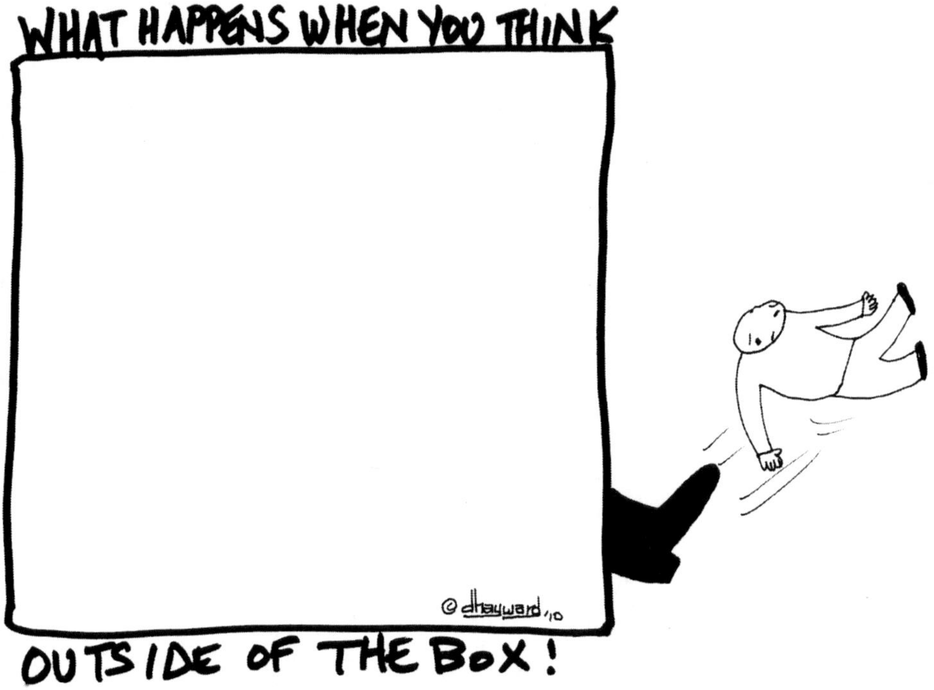
WHAT HAPPENS WHEN YOU THINK
© dhayward '10
OUTSIDE OF THE BOX!

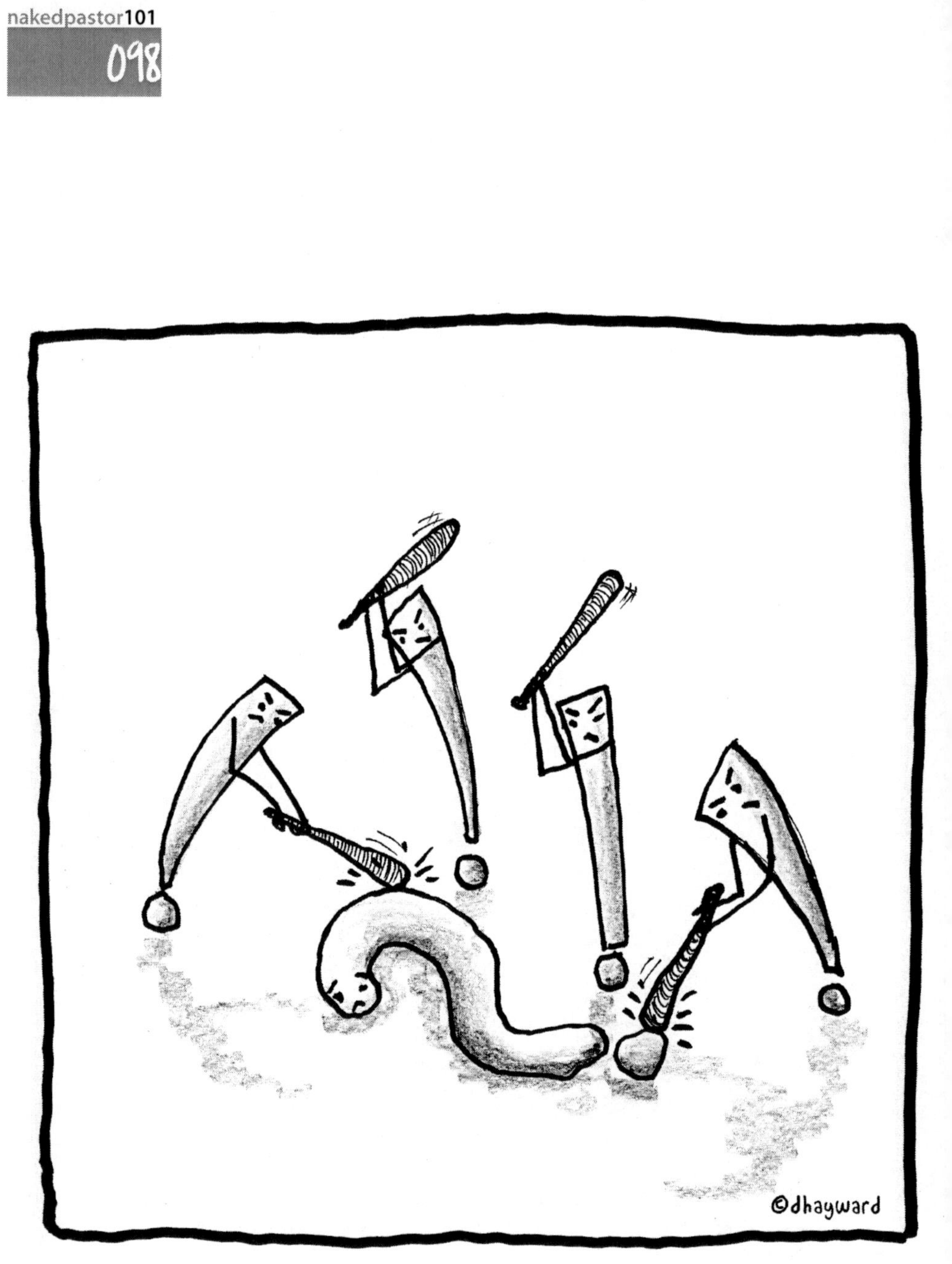
©dhayward

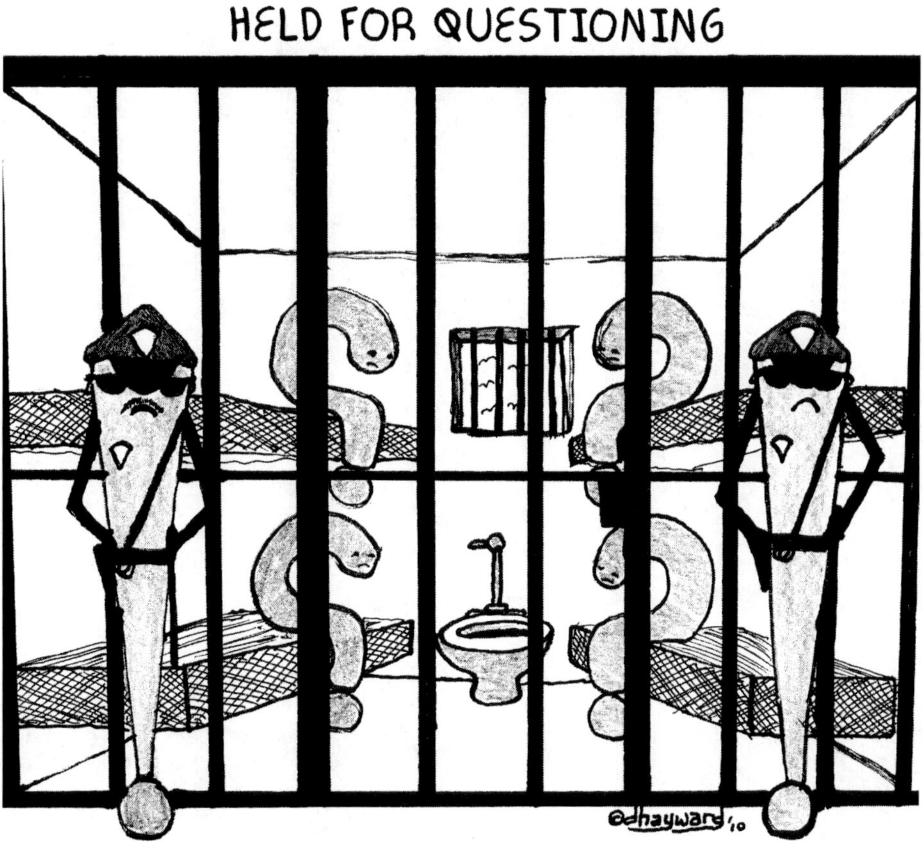
HELD FOR QUESTIONING
@dhayward '10

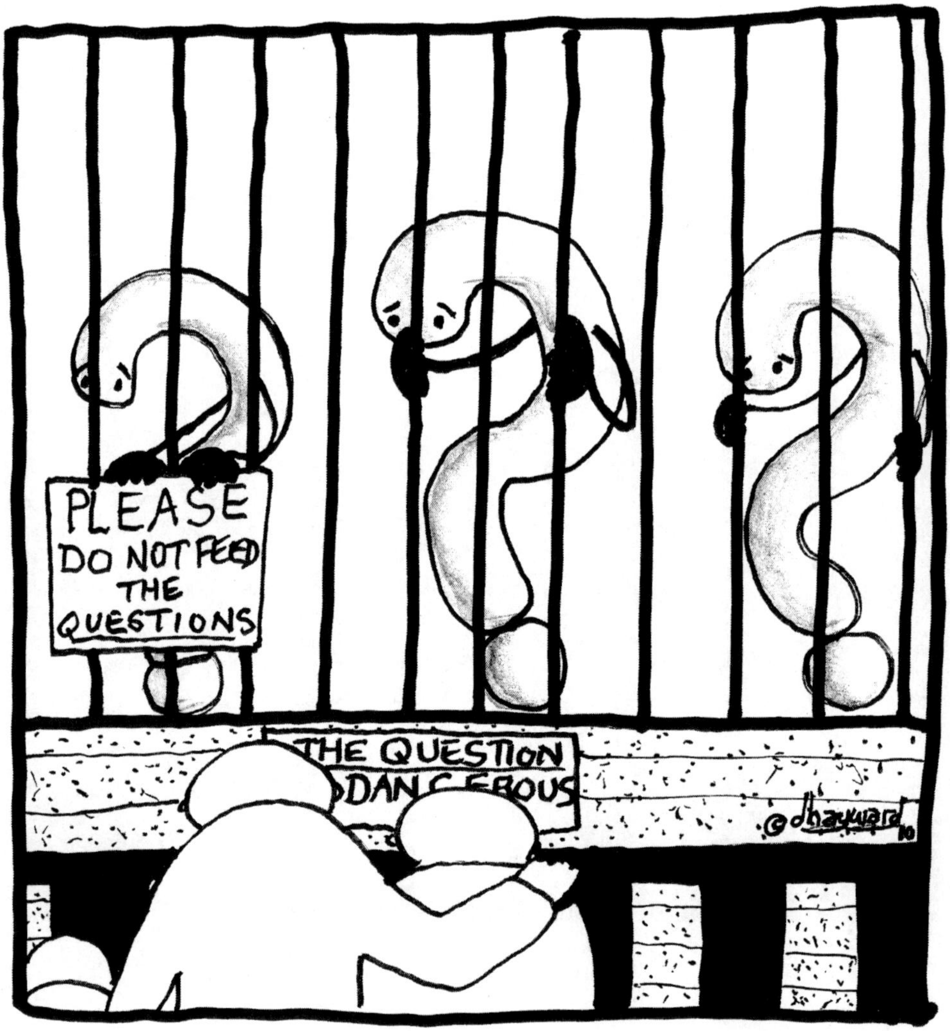
PLEASE
DO NOT FEED
THE
QUESTIONS
THE QUESTION
©dhayward 10

101

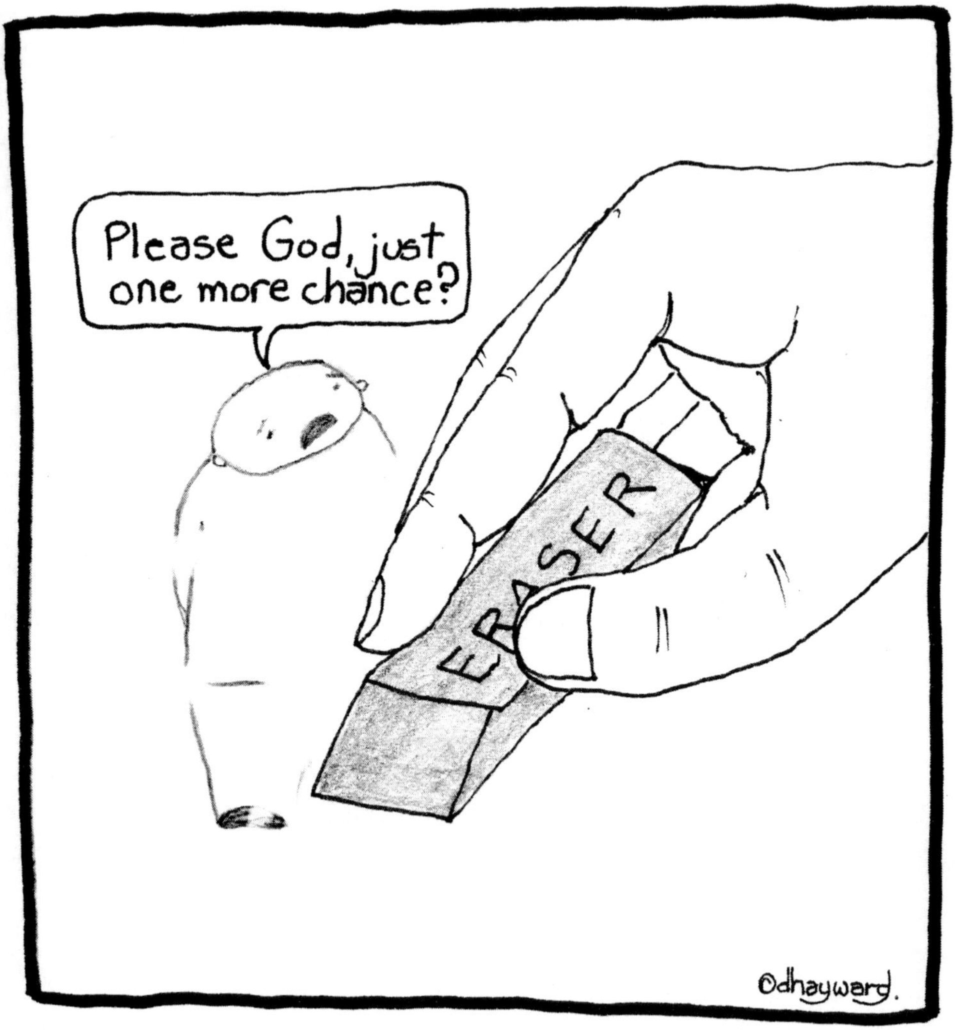
Please God, just one more chance?
ERASER
©dhayward.

Made in United States
North Haven, CT
09 September 2024